New
Ninja Dual Zone
Air Fryer Cookbook UK

1800 Days Crispy and Healthy Ninja Foodi Recipes for
Beginners with Tips & Tricks to Fry, Grill, and Bake (UK
Measurements & Ingredients)

Marie H. Scarberry

Contents

Chapter 6: Vegan and Vegetarian Recipes

Chapter 7: Family favourites 73

Introduction

In the midst of my culinary journey, I found myself at a fascinating crossroads where my love for vegetarian cuisine intersected with my diverse background as a former owner of a renowned non-vegetarian restaurant. As an advocate for vegetarian living, I sought to weave my expertise in both plant-based and non-vegetarian cooking into a harmonious tapestry, inspiring others to explore the flavoursome world of compassionate cuisine.

Word of my culinary prowess began to spread throughout the local community, and soon I found myself engaging in various events and gatherings dedicated to promoting sustainable and ethical eating practices. Local organisations and food enthusiasts recognized my passion and dedication to vegetarianism, inviting me to host cooking demonstrations and give talks on the transformative power of plant-based cooking.

It was during one such event that serendipity struck. Amidst a bustling farmers market, I stumbled upon a booth showcasing the legendary Ninja Dual Zone Air Fryer. The vendors, having heard of my culinary background, were eager for me to experience the wonders of this remarkable appliance. Little did I know that this encounter would forever change the course of my culinary journey. As I unboxed the Ninja Dual Zone Air Fryer, a rush of anticipation coursed through me. Its sleek design and multifunctional features exuded an air of possibility. Little did I know that this powerful appliance would become the catalyst for a newfound appreciation of plant-based cooking and a reimagining of familiar non-vegetarian dishes. Intrigued by the endless culinary avenues this air fryer promised, I embarked on a gastronomic exploration that bridged the realms of vegetarian and non-vegetarian fare. I delved into the art of creating crispy, golden tofu nuggets that satisfied even the most discerning palates. The air fryer's transformative powers allowed me to elevate vegetables like never before, coaxing out their inherent flavours and textures in ways that left me in awe.

News of my foray into the world of air frying with the Ninja Dual Zone Air Fryer quickly spread throughout the local food scene. Esteemed chefs, local media, and food critics took notice of my innovative approach to cooking and my dedication to advocating for compassionate and sustainable cuisine. I was invited to collaborate on projects and featured in local publications, which further fueled my passion to share my culinary insights with a wider audience.

Embracing the role of a local culinary ambassador, I started hosting cooking workshops and partnering with local farmers and producers to showcase the incredible variety of plant-based ingredients available in our community. The Ninja Dual Zone Air Fryer became the centrepiece of these culinary experiences, enchanting attendees with its ability to transform simple ingredients into mouth-watering creations. As my local engagement and recognition grew, so did my commitment to creating a cookbook that captured the essence of my culinary journey. This cookbook, infused with recipes inspired by my community's rich tapestry of flavours, pays homage to the local farmers, artisans, and food enthusiasts who have supported and inspired me along the way.

With each dish that graces the pages of this book, I celebrate the vibrancy of our local ingredients, honour the diversity of our culinary traditions, and encourage readers to embark on their own culinary explorations. The Ninja Dual Zone Air Fryer serves as a guiding light, enabling me to showcase the incredible flavours and textures that can be achieved with plant-based ingredients while honouring the roots of non-vegetarian cuisine.

This cookbook, a testament to my extraordinary journey, seeks to inspire fellow cooking enthusiasts to embark on their own adventure with the Ninja Dual Zone Air Fryer. With a tapestry of recipes that traverse the realms of vegetarian and non-vegetarian cuisine, it celebrates the art of compassionate cooking and the joys of embracing diverse culinary traditions.

Come, join me on this gastronomic odyssey as we unlock the immense potential of the Ninja Dual Zone Air Fryer, crafting delectable vegetarian masterpieces and reimagining non-vegetarian classics with a newfound sense of purpose and creativity!

All about the Ninja Dual Zone Air Fryer

Ninja Dual Zone Air Fryer is an extraordinary culinary marvel that is set to revolutionise your cooking experience: the Ninja Dual Zone Air Fryer. Prepare to embark on a culinary journey like no other, as this remarkable kitchen appliance combines advanced technology with unparalleled convenience, allowing you to create delectable meals with precision and ease.

1. Dual-Zone Cooking System:
The Ninja Dual Zone Air Fryer is equipped with an innovative dual-zone cooking system that allows you to independently control and customise two separate cooking zones within the appliance. This means you can simultaneously cook different dishes or ingredients without any flavour transfer. Each cooking zone has its own dedicated heating element and fan, ensuring precise temperature control and optimal cooking results for each zone.

2. Precision Air Circulation:
At the core of the Ninja Dual Zone Air Fryer is its precision air circulation technology. This advanced feature ensures even and rapid distribution of hot air throughout the cooking chamber. The powerful fans circulate the hot air in a controlled manner, cooking the food from all angles and producing crispy, golden exteriors while retaining moisture and tenderness inside. This results in perfectly cooked dishes with delightful textures and flavours.

3. Spacious Cooking Capacity:
The Ninja Dual Zone Air Fryer offers a generous cooking capacity, allowing you to prepare larger quantities of food to accommodate your family or guests. The spacious cooking chamber provides ample room to spread out the ingredients, ensuring even cooking and consistent results. Whether you're cooking for a small gathering or a big family meal, the Ninja Dual Zone Air Fryer has you covered.

4. Intuitive Controls and Preset Programs:
Operating the Ninja Dual Zone Air Fryer is a breeze thanks to its user-friendly interface and intuitive controls. The appliance features easy-to-read digital displays, allowing you to adjust temperature, time, and cooking settings with precision. Additionally, it offers preset programs for popular dishes, taking the guesswork out of cooking and ensuring consistent results every time.

5. Easy Cleanup and Maintenance:
Cleaning up after cooking is effortless with the Ninja Dual Zone Air Fryer. The non-stick surfaces of the cooking chamber and accessories prevent food from sticking, making them easy to clean with a gentle wipe. The removable parts are dishwasher-safe, allowing for convenient and thorough cleaning. Spend less time on cleanup and more time enjoying your delicious creations.

Main Features of your Ninja Dual Zone

With its versatile functions and customizable cooking zones, the Ninja Dual Zone Air Fryer provides endless culinary possibilities. Explore the world of air frying, roasting, baking, dehydrating, and reheating with this exceptional kitchen appliance.

1. Air Frying Function:

The air frying function of the Ninja Dual Zone Air Fryer allows you to achieve crispy and delicious results using hot air circulation. This function is perfect for cooking a wide range of dishes, including:
- French fries and potato wedges
- Chicken wings and drumsticks
- Breaded or battered foods like onion rings and mozzarella sticks
- Vegetable chips and roasted vegetables

2. Roasting Function:

With the roasting function, you can achieve succulent and perfectly cooked meats and vegetables with ease. This function is ideal for preparing:
- Roasted chicken, turkey, or pork
- Seasoned vegetables like Brussels sprouts, cauliflower, or carrots
- Roasted potatoes or sweet potatoes
- Whole or stuffed peppers, tomatoes, or mushrooms

3. Baking Function:

The baking function of the Ninja Dual Zone Air Fryer opens up a world of baking possibilities without the need for a traditional oven. You can bake a variety of items, such as:
- Muffins, cupcakes, and cakes
- Cookies and biscuits
- Pies and tarts
- Breads and rolls

4. Dehydrating Function:

The dehydrating function allows you to easily make homemade dried fruits, jerky, and more. It's perfect for preserving and enjoying seasonal fruits or making healthy snacks, such as:
- Apple chips and banana chips
- Dried herbs and spices
- Beef or turkey jerky
- Fruit leather or fruit roll-ups

5. Reheating Function:

The reheating function of the Ninja Dual Zone Air Fryer ensures that your leftovers or pre-cooked meals are heated evenly and retain their original texture and flavour. You can use this function to reheat a variety of dishes, such as:
- Pizza slices
- Casseroles and pasta dishes
- Fried foods like chicken tenders or spring rolls
- Sandwiches or wraps

6. Customizable Cooking Zones:

The Ninja Dual Zone Air Fryer features two independent cooking zones, allowing you to cook different dishes simultaneously without any flavour transfer. This is ideal for preparing meals with different cooking times or temperature requirements. For example:
- Crispy chicken wings in one zone while roasting vegetables in the other
- Baking a cake in one zone while dehydrating fruits in the other
- Air frying French fries in one zone while reheating pizza in the other

How to Clean & Maintenance

By following these cleaning and maintenance practices, you can keep your Ninja Dual Zone Air Fryer in excellent condition, ensuring its longevity and optimal performance. Enjoy cooking delicious meals with ease and convenience, knowing that your air fryer is clean and well-maintained. Follow these steps for effective cleaning and maintenance:

1. Unplug and Cool Down: Before starting the cleaning process, always unplug your air fryer from the power source and allow it to cool down completely.

2. Removable Parts: The Ninja Dual Zone Air Fryer features removable parts that are dishwasher-safe for easy cleaning. These typically include the cooking basket, crisper plate, and accessories. Remove these parts from the air fryer and wash them using warm, soapy water or place them in the dishwasher. Ensure thorough drying before reassembly.

3. Non-Stick Surfaces: Wipe down the interior and exterior surfaces of the air fryer using a damp cloth or sponge. Avoid using abrasive cleaners, steel wool, or harsh chemicals that can damage the non-stick coating.

4. Cleaning the Heating Element and Fan: Gently remove any food particles or residue that may have accumulated on the heating element or fan. Use a soft brush or a damp cloth to wipe these areas. Take caution not to immerse the air fryer's main unit in water or expose it to excessive moisture.

5. Air Vent: The air vent is located on the back of the air fryer and allows for proper ventilation. Ensure that it remains clear of any debris or obstructions to maintain optimal airflow.

Dos and Don'ts:

- Do clean the removable parts after each use to prevent buildup and ensure optimal hygiene.
- Do use mild, non-abrasive cleaning agents or dishwashing detergent when washing the removable parts.
- Do dry all parts thoroughly before reassembling and storing the air fryer.
- Don't immerse the main unit in water or any liquid. It is an electrical appliance and should be kept away from moisture.
- Don't use metal utensils or abrasive cleaning tools that can damage the non-stick coating.
- Don't use harsh chemicals or oven cleaners to clean the air fryer.

Maintenance Frequency:
- Clean the removable parts, including the cooking basket and accessories, after each use.
- Wipe down the interior and exterior surfaces of the air fryer regularly to remove any splatters or

spills.
- Clean the heating element and fan as needed, especially if there are visible food particles or residue.
- Check and clear the air vent periodically to ensure proper ventilation.

Tips and Tricks for the Ninja Dual Zone Air Fryer

These tips and tricks will help you make the most of your Ninja Dual Zone Air Fryer and explore the delicious possibilities it offers. Happy cooking and enjoy creating mouthwatering dishes for yourself, your family, and your friends! Here are some helpful tips and tricks to enhance your cooking experience with the Ninja Dual Zone Air Fryer. The tips are categorised and numbered for easy reference:

1. Preheating:
- Preheat the air fryer before adding your ingredients. This helps to ensure even cooking and crispy results.

2. Proper Air Circulation:
- Avoid overcrowding the cooking zones. Leave enough space between food items to allow for proper air circulation and even cooking.

3. Shake and Flip:
- Shake or flip your food halfway through the cooking process to ensure even browning and crispiness.

4. Cooking Time and Temperature:
- Adjust the cooking time and temperature based on the desired level of crispness and the thickness of the ingredients. Thicker cuts may require longer cooking times.

5. Layering:
- For dishes that require different cooking times, consider layering the ingredients. Place those that require less cooking time on top to prevent overcooking.

6. Seasoning and Marinades:

- Season or marinate your ingredients before air frying to infuse them with flavor. Experiment with different spices, herbs, and marinades to enhance the taste of your dishes.

7. Oil Spraying:

- For added crispiness, lightly spray or brush a thin layer of oil on your ingredients before air frying. This can be done using a cooking oil spray or a brush.

8. Parchment Paper or Foil:

- Use parchment paper or aluminium foil to line the air fryer basket or cooking zones when cooking sticky or delicate foods like fish or certain vegetables. This helps to prevent sticking and makes cleanup easier.

9. Reheating Leftovers:

- Use the air fryer's reheating function to revive leftovers. It can help restore the crispness of foods like fries, chicken tenders, or even pizza slices.

10. Experiment with Recipes:

- Don't be afraid to try new recipes and experiment with different ingredients in your Ninja Dual Zone Air Fryer. It's a versatile appliance that can handle a wide range of dishes, from appetisers to main courses and even desserts.

11. Keep an Eye on the Food:

- Check on your food periodically during the cooking process to prevent overcooking or burning. Adjust the cooking time or temperature if necessary.

12. Clean and Maintain Regularly:

- Follow the cleaning and maintenance instructions provided to keep your air fryer in top condition. A clean appliance ensures optimal performance and longevity.

13. Always refer to the manufacturer's manual and guidelines for specific recommendations and safety instructions related to your Ninja Dual Zone Air Fryer.

Frequently-Asked FAQs

1. Cooking and Functions:

a. How does the air frying function work?
- The air frying function uses hot air circulated at high speed to cook food quickly and evenly, creating a crispy texture without excessive oil.

b. Can I cook multiple dishes at the same time using the dual zones?
- Yes, the dual zones allow you to cook separate dishes simultaneously, each with their own temperature and time settings.

c.. Is it possible to roast meats and vegetables in the air fryer?
- Absolutely! The air fryer is suitable for roasting meats, poultry, and vegetables, giving them a delicious, caramelised exterior.

d. Can I use the air fryer for dehydrating fruits and making jerky?
- While the air fryer is not specifically designed for dehydration, you can use it at low temperatures to dehydrate certain foods like fruits or make jerky.

e. Does the air fryer have a reheating function?
- Yes, the air fryer typically includes a reheating function that allows you to quickly and efficiently reheat leftovers to their desired temperature.

2. Cleaning and Maintenance:

a. Are the removable parts dishwasher-safe?
- Yes, the removable parts such as the cooking basket and accessories are generally dishwasher-safe for convenient cleaning.

b. Can I submerge the main unit in water for cleaning?
- No, the main unit should never be submerged in water or any liquid. Use a damp cloth or sponge to clean the exterior.

c. How do I clean the heating element and fan?
- Gently remove any food particles or residue from the heating element and fan using a soft brush or a damp cloth.

d. Is it necessary to clean the air vent? How often?
- Yes, it is important to keep the air vent clear of

any debris or obstructions for proper ventilation. Clean it as needed, especially if you notice reduced airflow.

3. Safety:
a. Is the Ninja Dual Zone Air Fryer safe to use?
- Yes, the air fryer is designed with safety features such as auto shut-off, cool-touch handles, and non-slip feet to ensure safe operation.
b. Can I leave the air fryer unattended during cooking?
- It is generally recommended not to leave the air fryer unattended during cooking for safety reasons. It is best to monitor the cooking process.
c. Are the exterior surfaces of the air fryer hot during operation?
- The exterior surfaces may become warm during operation, but they are designed to stay relatively cool to the touch to prevent burns.
d. Can I use metal utensils in the air fryer?
- It is advised to use non-metal utensils, such as silicone, wood, or plastic, to avoid scratching the non-stick coating of the air fryer basket.

4. Troubleshooting:
a. Why is the food not cooking evenly?
- Uneven cooking may occur if the food is overcrowded or the air vents are blocked. Ensure proper airflow and avoid overcrowding for even cooking results.
b. My air fryer is not turning on. What should I do?
- Check if the air fryer is properly plugged in and the power source is working. If the issue persists, refer to the troubleshooting section of the manual or contact customer support.
c. The air fryer is producing smoke. Is it normal?
- Light smoke or steam may be produced during cooking, especially when cooking high-fat foods. Ensure proper ventilation and monitor the cooking process.
d. Why is there a strange odour during cooking?
- A slight odour during initial uses is normal and should dissipate. If the odour persists or is unusual,

check for any food debris or residues that may need cleaning.

5. Anything missing?
a. Are there any additional accessories available for the Ninja Dual Zone Air Fryer?
- Yes, Ninja may offer additional accessories like baking pans, racks, or skewers for more cooking options. Check their official website or product listings for compatible accessories.
b. Can I use third-party accessories with the air fryer?
- It is recommended to use genuine Ninja accessories for optimal performance and safety. The compatibility of third-party accessories may vary, so refer to the manufacturer's guidelines.
c. Does the air fryer come with a warranty?
- Yes, the air fryer typically comes with a manufacturer's warranty. Refer to the product packaging or manual for warranty details.

Book Summary

With a heart full of flavours and a passion for culinary harmony, this cookbook serves as a delightful compendium of recipes that bridge the realms of vegetarian and non-vegetarian cooking. Divided into six captivating chapters, it invites readers to embark on a culinary adventure that celebrates the diverse flavours and textures of compassionate cuisine.

Chapter 1: Breakfast Recipes awakens the senses with an array of mouthwatering morning delights, from omelette to shakshuka, pancakes to burritos. Each recipe is carefully crafted to infuse the start of your day with nourishment and energy.

Chapter 2: Beans & Grains Recipes explores the versatility of plant-based proteins, offering creative and hearty dishes that showcase the wonders of legumes and grains. From comforting lentil burgers to aromatic quinoa salads, these recipes will inspire you to elevate your meals to new heights.

Chapter 3: Meat & Chicken Recipes introduces

a selection of innovative dishes that reimagine familiar non-vegetarian favourites. With the magic of the air fryer, succulent cuts of meat and chicken are transformed into crispy delights that tantalise the taste buds and demonstrate that compassionate cooking knows no boundaries.

Chapter 4: Fish and Seafood Recipes invites you to dive into a world of culinary exploration, where delicate flavours of the ocean are celebrated. From flaky air-fried fish fillets to zesty seafood pilau, these recipes bring the coastal charm to your plate with a cruelty-free twist.

Chapter 5: Snacks and Appetizer Recipes tempts the palate with a collection of tantalising bites and finger foods. Whether you're hosting a gathering or simply indulging in self-care, these appetisers, from Chinese spring rolls to Greek feta cheese salad, are sure to impress.

Chapter 6: Vegan & Vegetarian Recipes takes centre stage, showcasing the full potential of plant-based cooking. From vibrant salads bursting with fresh produce to comforting plant-powered main courses, these recipes celebrate the abundance and nourishment that come from embracing a vegan and vegetarian lifestyle.

Chapter 7 : Family Favourites - dishes that are loved and enjoyed by all members of the family. No matter which family favourite recipe you choose to prepare, the most important thing is that it provides a sense of comfort and warmth that brings family members together.

Through this cookbook, I invite you to join me on a culinary journey that transcends dietary boundaries, celebrates local ingredients, and champions the art of compassionate cooking. With the Ninja Dual Zone Air Fryer as our trusted companion, we embark on a flavorful adventure that proves delicious food can be both ethical and sensational. Embrace the possibilities, savour the flavours, and let this cookbook be your guide as you explore the remarkable world of vegetarian and non-vegetarian cooking with the Ninja Dual Zone Air Fryer!

Chapter 1: Breakfast Recipes

Air Fryer Shakshuka

Servings: 2
Prep time: 11 mins / Cook time: 20 mins

Ingredients
- 200g chopped tomatoes (canned)
- Paprika
- Chilli flakes (optional)
- 20 Orange peppers (chopped finely)
- Cumin
- Salt and pepper as desired
- 1 finely diced garlic clove
- 2 eggs

For the Topping
- 30g crushed feta cheese
- Chopped coriander
- ½ red Chilli

Preparation Procedure
1. Preheat your Ninja Dual Zone Air Fryer to 1600C on any zone preferred, Zone 1, 2 or both simultaneously.
2. Put the canned tomatoes (chopped), paprika, garlic, chilli flakes, onion powder, salt, pepper, cumin and diced pepper into a shallow oven-resistant dish.
3. Mix the Ingredients in the oven-resistant dish properly to incorporate the spices.
4. Taking 2 spoons, make a well in the vegetable mixture and crack the 2 eggs into it.
5. Put the mixture together with the dish into the Ninja Dual Zone Air Fryer drawers depending on the zone that's been preheated. Leaving the temperature at 160C, its preheated temperature value.
6. Bake for 20 mins or until to eggs are baked enough to your preferred consistency in the air fryer,
7. Garnish your Shakshuka dish with coriander, feta cheese and/or chilli. Enjoy with some crusty bread.

Eggs On Toast

Servings: 2
Prep time: 5 mins / Cook Time: 8 mins

Ingredients
- 2 slices of white bread
- 2 Medium-sized Eggs
- 25g Butter or any spread of your choice
- Salt and Pepper as preferred
- Sriracha Sauce

Preparation Procedure:
1. Spray the non stick air fryer plates with little oil and place the slices of bread on it.
2. Form a well in the middle of the slices of bread by taking a round mug and using its base to push down into the middle of the bread.
3. Crack open the eggs and pour them into the well. Season to taste with salt and pepper.
4. Spread butter or your preferred spread on the outside of the well formed on each of the bread slices.
5. Turn on the Ninja Dual Zone air fryer and sync both zones.
6. Preheat your air fryer machine for 5 mins before air frying.
7. Place your Bread and eggs on the non stick plates in the air fryer drawers and set the temperature.
8. Set to air fry for about 7-8 minutes depending on how cooked you prefer the egg yolk.
9. Take it out the airfryer when the timer is over.
10. For toppings, drizzle on some sriracha sauce on top and serve.

Air Fryer French Toast Sticks

Servings: 2
Prep time: 7 mins / Cook Time: 9 mins

Ingredients
- 1 small sized loaf of white bread
- 2 Medium-sized Eggs
- Milk
- Cinnamon and Sugar to your taste
- Vanilla Extract

- Maple Syrup, Honey or any other topping of your choice.

Preparation Procedure:
1. Using a serrated knife, cut the loaf of bread into strips and set aside.
2. In a shallow dish, whisk together eggs, milk and vanilla extract.
3. Mix the cinnamon and sugar in a different shallow dish and set aside.
4. Dip each bread strip into the egg mixture, evenly coating it.
5. After dipping each bread stick into the egg mixture, dip next into the dry mixture, i.e the sugar and cinnamon mixture.
6. Spray some oil on the non-stick plates of your Ninja Dual Zone Air Fryer and place the coated bread sticks on the plates. Allow some space of about an inch to two between the bread sticks.
7. Place the non stick plates into the air fryer drawers and turn on your Air Fryer.
8. Select the "AIR FRY" option and airfry at 175°C for 5 minutes, flip the sticks, and cook for 3-4 minutes.
9. Remove from the air fryer and serve with maple syrup, honey or your favorite toppings.

Air Fryer Breakfast Burritos:

Servings: 2
Prep time: 20 mins / Cook Time: 10 mins

Ingredients
- Ground Chicken
- Ground Sausage
- 1 Diced Potatoes (Red or Yellowish)
- 1 large Yellow, Red and Green Bell Peppers, all diced
- 28g of Shredded Cheese
- ½ Onions bulb, Red and Sweet cut in rings
- 2 Eggs
- Olive Oil
- ⅛ tablespoon of Black Pepper
- Salt to taste
- 2 tbsp Butter
- Garlic Powder
- Tortillas (10-inch sized)
- Salsa or Sour Cream

Preparation Procedure:
1. Preheat the Ninja Dual Zone Air Fryer to 350°F (175°C).
2. While you preheat the Air Fryer, melt 2 tablespoonfuls of butter in 3 tablespoonfuls of olive oil separately in a saucepan over medium heat.
3. Add in the diced potatoes, stir and cook for 7-8 mins, then add the onion rings and diced peppers.
4. Saute this for 4 minutes more, then remove it from heat and set it aside.
5. Cook the ground chicken and sausage with spices to your taste, drain and set it aside.
6. In a bowl, beat eggs and season with salt and pepper.
7. Heat a frying pan over medium heat and scramble the eggs until cooked.
8. Place a tortilla on a flat surface and add a spoonful of scrambled eggs, cooked sausage and chicken, sauteed potatoes, shredded cheese, and any other desired fillings.
9. Fold the sides of the tortilla inward and roll it tightly.
10. Lightly spray the burrito with cooking spray and place it seam-side down in the Ninja Dual Zone Air Fryer drawers.
11. Cook for 8-10 minutes until the tortilla is crispy and golden. Serve with salsa or sour cream.

Air Fryer Egg Cups

Servings: 2
Prep time: 3 mins / Cook Time: 12 mins

Ingredients
- 2 large sized Eggs
- Salt and Pepper as preferred
- 40g Ham or Bacon
- Shredded Cheese
- ½ Onions bulb
- Mushrooms
- 3 Tbsp Milk (optional)
- Preferred spices

Preparation Procedure
1. Preheat the Ninja Dual Zone Air fryer to 325°F (165°C).
2. Spray muffin cups with cooking spray.
3. Dice up all the fillings, i.e. the ham or bacon,

whichever you choose, the onions, mushrooms etc.

4. Line each cup with some ham or bacon.
5. Crack an egg into each cup, careful not to break the yolk. You can also choose to whisk the egg before you put it in. Take your pick.
6. Put in the mushrooms, onions and any other additional fillings you've chosen
7. Season with salt, pepper, and any desired herbs or spices.
8. Add the shredded cheese as toppings.
9. Place the muffin tin into your Ninja Dual Zone Air Fryer drawers.
10. Set it to cook for 8-10 minutes, or until the eggs are set to your liking.
11. Ensure the cheese is well melted and the cups are golden brown around the edges.
12. Press the egg cup down, and it's cooked enough when it bounces back to shape or is puffy.
13. Carefully remove the egg cups from the air fryer and serve hot.

Air Fryer Banana Pancakes

Servings: 2
Prep time: 18 mins / Cook Time: 8 mins

Ingredients
- 1 large ripe banana
- I large egg
- ½ tablespoon of cooking oil (vegetable, avocado or coconut oil)
- 200g Flour
- 120g Sugar
- 1 tsp Baking powder
- Milk
- A pinch of salt
- Lemon juice / Buttermilk (optional)

Preparation Procedure
1. In a bowl, mash ripe banana until smooth. Ensure the banana is super ripe to add sweetness and depth to the pancake. Press into the banana using a fork and mash thoroughly.
2. Add egg and combine thoroughly with the mashed bananas. Do this until you have a smooth mixture.
3. Add the flour, baking powder, milk, and a pinch

of salt to the bowl and mix until well combined.

4. To get your pancakes fluffy, increase the acidity of the pancake mix. You can get this with the addition of lemon juice or using buttermilk as it is also acidic
5. Turn on your Ninja Dual Zone Air Fryer and select the "AIR FRY" option.
6. Preheat the Ninja Dual Zone Air Fryer to 175°C.
7. Lightly grease the air fryer basket or use parchment paper.
8. Spoon small portions of the pancake batter onto the prepared basket.
9. Cook for 4-5 minutes, flip the pancakes, and cook for 2-3 minutes.
10. Serve the pancakes warm with your favorite toppings.

Air Fryer Breakfast Sausages

Servings: 2
Prep time: 3 mins / Cook Time: 10 mins

Ingredients
- Sausage links

Preparation Procedure
1. Preheat the Ninja Dual Zone Air Fryer to 200°C.
2. Place down some parchment paper on the non-stick plates to aid easy cleaning. Poke a couple of holes in the paper to aid easy circulation in the air fryer.
3. Place the sausages on the non-stick plates covered with parchment paper and in a single layer in your Ninja Dual Zone Air fryer basket.
4. Depending on the thickness of your sausage, the time you need to cook it might vary. Cook for 8-10 minutes for regular sized sausages and about 10-14 minutes for thicker sausages.
5. Flip them halfway through the time for even browning.
6. Check for doneness and cook for 2-3 minutes if needed.
7. If the sausages are not fully cooked, continue air frying for 2 to 3 minutes until they reach the desired internal temperature.
8. Once cooked, carefully remove the sausages from the air fryer using tongs or a spatula. Be cautious as they will be hot.

9. Place the cooked sausages on a plate lined with paper towels to absorb any excess grease.
10. Let the sausages cool for a few minutes before serving.

Air Fryer Cinnamon Rolls

Servings: 2
Prep time: 3 mins / Cook Time: 8 mins

Ingredients:
- 1 package of refrigerated cinnamon roll dough (with icing)
- 2 tablespoons melted butter
- 50g of granulated sugar
- 1 tablespoon ground cinnamon
- Cooking spray or oil for greasing

Preparation Procedures:
1. Preheat your Ninja Dual Zone Air Fryer to 175°C for about 5 minutes.
2. Take out the cinnamon roll dough and separate the individual rolls.
3. Lightly grease the air fryer drawer with cooking spray or oil to prevent sticking.
4. Place the cinnamon rolls in a single layer in the air fryer drawer, leaving some space between them for expansion.
5. Brush the melted butter evenly over the tops of the cinnamon rolls.
6. In a small bowl, combine the granulated sugar and ground cinnamon. Mix well to create the cinnamon-sugar mixture.
7. Sprinkle the cinnamon-sugar mixture over the buttered cinnamon rolls, ensuring they are evenly coated.
8. Place the filled air fryer drawer into the preheated air fryer.
9. Select the "AIR FRY" option and air fry the cinnamon rolls at 175°C for about 8 to 10 minutes or until golden brown and cooked through.
10. Once cooked, carefully remove the cinnamon rolls from the air fryer using tongs or a spatula.
11. Allow the cinnamon rolls to cool slightly before icing them. Drizzle the included icing from the package over the warm cinnamon rolls.
12. Serve the air fryer cinnamon rolls immediately and enjoy!

Air Fryer Mini Frittatas

Servings: 2
Prep time: 6 mins / Cook Time: 12 mins

Ingredients:
- 6 large eggs
- 59g milk
- 56g shredded cheese (cheddar, mozzarella, or your choice)
- 37g diced bell peppers
- 29g diced onions
- 35g diced cooked ham or bacon (optional)
- Salt and pepper to taste
- Cooking spray or olive oil for greasing

Preparation Procedures
1. Preheat your air fryer to 350°F (175°C) for about 5 minutes.
2. In a mixing bowl, whisk the eggs and milk until well combined. Season with salt and pepper according to your taste.
3. Add the shredded cheese, diced bell peppers, onions, and cooked ham or bacon (if using) to the egg mixture. Stir well to evenly distribute the ingredients.
4. Lightly grease the wells of a mini muffin tin with cooking spray or olive oil.
5. Spoon the egg mixture into the mini muffin tin wells, filling each one about 3/4 full. Be careful not to overfill as the frittatas will rise slightly during cooking.
6. Once the air fryer is preheated, carefully place the filled mini muffin tin in the air fryer basket. If your air fryer has a rack accessory, you can use it to create more space for air circulation.
7. Cook the frittatas in the air fryer at 350°F (175°C) for 10 to 12 minutes, or until the tops are set and lightly golden. You can check for doneness by inserting a toothpick or a knife into the center of one frittata – if it comes out clean, they are ready.
8. Once cooked, remove the mini muffin tin from the air fryer and let it cool for a few minutes. The frittatas will slightly deflate as they cool.
9. Use a butter knife or a small spatula to gently loosen the edges of the frittatas from the muffin

tin. Carefully lift them out and transfer to a serving plate.

10. Serve the mini frittatas warm as a delicious and convenient breakfast or brunch option. They can also be refrigerated in an airtight container for up to 3 days and reheated in the microwave or air fryer before serving.

Breakfast Quesadillas

Servings: 2
Prep time: 4 mins / Cook Time: 8 mins

Ingredients:
- Tortillas
- 2 Eggs
- 50g Cheese
- Sour Cream, Guacamole etc

Preparation Procedures:
1. Preheat your Ninja Dual Zone Air Fryer at 175 degrees Celsius. That is the perfect temperature for cooking quesadillas.
2. Take out your fry pan and scramble-fry your eggs for the filling. Set this aside when you're done.
3. Take out the tortillas and place them on a clean and flat surface.
4. Prepare your fillings, i.e. the scrambled eggs, and cheese. Spread the scrambled eggs on one half of the tortilla flat.
5. Sprinkle the other half with cheese and fold the tortilla in half.
6. Prepare your Ninja Dual Zone Air Fryer drawers by spraying the non-stick plates with cooking spray or using parchment paper. This will prevent the tortillas from sticking and would aid easy cleaning too.
7. Arrange the quesadillas with enough space in between them on the non-stick plates. The space in between is to ensure the quesadillas cook evenly.
8. Place a heavy oven resistant object or even stick toothpicks down the quesadillas to keep the tortillas closed.
9. Select the "AIR FRY" option and airfry the quesadillas for about 8 minutes. The quesadillas are ready when the tortillas become golden brown and the cheese is melted.

10. Take the quesadillas out and serve with sour cream, guacamole, or any of your favorite cream toppings.

Air Fryer Avocado Toast

Servings: 2
Prep time: 5 mins / Cook Time: 3 mins

Ingredients:
- 1 Avocado
- 4 slices of Bread
- Lemon juice
- Minced Garlic
- 1 Tomato (Diced)
- Salt and Black Pepper to taste

Preparation Procedures:
1. Make a small bowl, mash up the avocado, salt, lemon juice, pepper and minced garlic. You can keep it lumpy or smooth, whichever consistency works for you.
2. Another alternative to making the avocado mixture is mashing just the avocado and lemon juice alone. Then add the spices when you spread the avocado mixture on the bread.
3. Toast your bread in the Ninja Dual Zone Air Fryer non-stick plates, place it in the drawers, set the air fryer to "ROAST" and set the temperature at 230 degrees Celsius. Toast the bread for 2-3 minutes
4. Spread the prepared avocado mixture and add more seasonings and the diced tomatoes if you wish. Place another slice on the avocado spread.
5. Place the prepared avocado toasts back into the air fryer basket and air fry for 1-2 minutes until the avocado spread and tomatoes are warmed.
6. Carefully remove the avocado toasts from the air fryer and transfer them to a serving plate.
7. Serve while it's still warm to enjoy.

Air Fryer Mini Quiches

Servings: 2
Prep time: 5 mins / Cook Time: 12 mins

Ingredients:
- 3 large eggs
- 39.5g milk
- 18.6g shredded cheese (such as cheddar or Gruyere)
- 35g diced cooked bacon or ham
- 35g Diced vegetables (such as bell peppers, spinach, or mushrooms)
- Salt and pepper to taste
- Cooking spray

Preparation Procedures:
1. Preheat your Ninja Dual Zone Air Fryer to 175°C for about 5 minutes.
2. In a mixing bowl, whisk the eggs and milk until well combined. Season with salt and pepper according to your taste.
3. Prepare your muffin tin or silicone muffin cups by lightly greasing them with cooking spray.
4. Distribute the diced bacon or ham, vegetables, and shredded cheese evenly among the cups in the muffin tin.
5. Pour the egg mixture into each cup, filling them about 3/4 of the way. Leave a little room at the top as the quiches will puff up while cooking.
6. Place the muffin tin in the preheated air fryer basket.
7. Cook the quiches in the air fryer at 175°C for approximately 10-12 minutes or until set and the tops are lightly golden brown. You can check for doneness by inserting a toothpick into the center of a quiche. If it comes out clean, they are ready.
8. Carefully remove the muffin tin from the air fryer using oven mitts or tongs, as it will be hot. Let the quiches cool in the tin for a few minutes before removing them.
9. Use a butter knife or small spatula to gently loosen the quiches from the muffin cups. They should come out easily.
10. Serve the mini quiches warm as a delicious breakfast or brunch option.

Air Fryer Breakfast Pizza

Servings: 2
Prep time: 5 mins / Cook Time: 8 mins

Ingredients:
- Crescent Dough
- Cheddar cheese
- Bacon
- Scrambled eggs
- Mozzarella cheese
- Cherry tomatoes, sliced in half
- Chopped green onion

Preparation Procedures:
1. Take out a springform pan or a silicone one of 8 inches wide in diameter and spray it with some non stick cooking spray or brush the pan with some olive oil.
2. Spread the ready made dough to the bottom of the pan, ensuring it is as flat as possible.
3. Turn on your Ninja Dual Zone Air Fryer, set it to "Bake" and its temperature at 176 degrees Celsius.
4. Place the pan into the Air Fryer drawer and bake for 5 minutes or until the top turns slightly brown.
5. Take the pan out from the air fryer and put the toppings on. Place your eggs, cheese, green onions, bacon and tomatoes and any additions of your choice.
6. Return the pan into the drawers at the same 175 degrees Celsius for another 5-8 minutes.
7. The pizza is ready when the top and the cheese turn golden brown.
8. Serve immediately while the toppings are still hot. At this point it should also have a crispy bottom and edges, all of which add to the pleasurable eating experience.

Air Fryer Hash Browns

Servings: 2
Prep time: 4 mins / Cook Time: 8 mins

Ingredients:
- Frozen Hash Brown Patties
- Salt to taste
- Garlic Powder
- Black Pepper to taste

Preparation Procedures:
1. Preheat the Air Fryer to a temperature of 200oC.
2. Place the hash brown patties on the preheated Air Fryer.
3. Ensure that you do not overlap the patties or make them stack upon placement. Place the hash brown patties in a single layer in the air fryer basket of one zone, ensuring not to overcrowd the basket. This will allow the air to circulate properly and ensure even cooking.
4. No need to spray or brush with oil as they're quite cooked already and will still have some oil on them.
5. Place in Zone 1 or Zone 2 in the Ninja Dual Zone Air Fryer. Set the timer for 15 minutes.
6. After 15 minutes, remove the hash brown patties from the air fryer. Use tongs or a spatula to carefully flip the hash brown patties. Return the zone to the air fryer.
7. If you prefer shredded hash browns, you can crumble them to get this result. Otherwise, serve the hash brown patties once they have turned a golden brown.

Baked Burrata Bruschetta

Serves 6
Prep time: 5 minutes / Cook time: 4 minutes

Ingredients:
- 1 loaf of crusty bread, sliced
- 500g cherry tomatoes, halved
- 1 large garlic clove, peeled
- 30ml extra-virgin olive oil
- 1 tbsp chardonnay vinegar
- Sea salt and ground black pepper, to taste
- 100g broad beans, double podded, blanched
- 1 large burrata, at room temperature and sliced
- 1 small pack fresh mint, chopped
- 1 small pack fresh parsley, chopped

Preparation Procedures:
1. Place bread slices in zone 1 and zone 2 drawers. Select zone 1 and pair it with "BAKE" at 180°C for 2 minutes. Select "MATCH" to duplicate settings across both zones. Press the "START/ STOP" button.
2. Meanwhile, toss cherry tomatoes with garlic, olive oil, vinegar, salt, black pepper, and beans.
3. Top the bread slices with tomato mixture and arrange them in both drawers.
4. Select zone 1 and pair it with "BAKE" at 180°C for 2 minutes. Select "MATCH" to duplicate settings across both zones. Press the "START/ STOP" button.
5. Garnish your bruschetta with fresh burrata, mint, and basil leaves.

Air Fryer Blueberry Muffins

Servings: 2
Prep time: 10 mins / Cook Time: 20 mins

Ingredients:
- 120g Flour
- 1 Egg
- 80ml Milk
- 1 tsp Vanilla
- 1 tsp Baking Powder
- 70g Sugar
- 85g Blueberries
- 2 Tbsp Vegetable oil

Preparation Procedures
1. Ensure the baking cups fit in a single Air Fryer drawer layer. When done, spray your muffin cups with non-stick cooking spray or smear with vegetable oil to prevent sticking.
2. Get a large mixing bowl, crack the eggs and pour in the sugar. Whisk thoroughly to combine them properly.
3. Pour in the vanilla extract, oil and milk, and mix well.
4. After mixing well and incorporating the ingredients, pour the flour and baking powder. Stir gently to get the best results.
5. When you're done mixing, put in the blueberries

and reserve some for topping the muffin.

6. Transfer the batter into the muffin cups and measure evenly using a spoon. This will ensure the muffins get ready at about the same time.

7. Sprinkle on the remaining blueberries on top of eac cup of batter and prepare to place in your Ninja Dual Zone Air Fryer.

8. Set the fryer to a temperature of 150 degrees Celsius, use the "BAKE" option on the Air Fryer and bake the muffins at 151 degrees Celsius for 20 minutes.

9. Dip a toothpick in to check for doneness and if it comes out clean, its ready.

10. Serve with a hot glass of cocoa or coffee to start your money.

Air Fryer Veggie Omelet

Servings: 2
Prep time: 4 mins / Cook Time: 10 mins

Ingredients:
- Eggs
- Onions
- Mushrooms
- Cherry Tomatoes (Chopped)
- Shredded cheese

Preparation Procedures
1. Preheat the Ninja Dual Zone Air Fryer to a temperature of 200oC.
2. Take out a bowl and break the eggs into it. Add salt and pepper exactly how you like it and keep whisking.
3. Put in the toppings, i.e. mushrooms, chopped tomatoes and onions.
4. Keep whisking the egg mixture lightly and pour it into an oil-brushed oven resistant pan. If you have some parchment paper, line your baking pan with it to aid cleaning and easy removal.
5. Set your Ninja Dual Zone Air to "Bake" and bake the eggs for 5 minutes, to get a nicely cooked fluffy omelet.
6. If you want a fairly firmer omelet, let it cook for about 6-7 minutes. Go 8-10 for a very solid and well-done omelet.
7. You can check the doneness by inserting a toothpick or a knife into the center; it should

come out clean.

8. Carefully remove the baking dish from the Air Fryer. Sprinkle the shredded cheese on top of the omelet while it's still hot, allowing it to melt.

9. Let the omelet cool for a few minutes before slicing it into wedges or squares. Garnish with fresh herbs, if desired.

Breakfast Sausage and Egg Sandwich

Servings: 2
Prep time: 10 mins / Cook Time: 8 mins

Ingredients:
- 4 breakfast sausage patties
- 4 large eggs
- 4 English muffins, split
- 4 slices of cheese (cheddar, American, or your preference)
- Salt and pepper to taste
- For the topping; sliced tomatoes, avocado, lettuce, ketchup, or hot sauce

Preparation Procedures:
1. Preheat your Ninja Dual Zone Air Fryer to 190°C for about 5 minutes.
2. Place the breakfast sausage patties in a single layer on the non-stick plates and put into the Air Fryer drawer. Cook for 7-10 minutes, flipping them halfway through, until they are browned and cooked.
3. While the sausage patties are cooking, crack the eggs into small bowls or ramekins. Season with salt and pepper to taste.
4. Remove the sausage patties from the Air Fryer and set them aside.
5. Place the individual bowls with the cracked eggs into the Air Fryer drawers using either Zone 1 or 2
6. Cook the eggs in the Air Fryer for about 5-6 minutes until the whites are set, and the yolks are still slightly runny. If you prefer fully cooked eggs, you can cook them longer.
7. Assemble the breakfast sandwiches. Place a cooked sausage patty on top of the cheese, followed by a cooked egg. Add any optional toppings you desire, such as sliced tomatoes,

avocado, lettuce, ketchup, or hot sauce.

8. Place the assembled sandwiches back in the Air Fryer for about 1-2 minutes until the cheese melts and the sandwiches are heated through.

9. Carefully remove the sandwiches from the Air Fryer and allow them to cool.

10. Serve the Breakfast Sausage and Egg Sandwiches hot and enjoy a satisfying and delicious breakfast!

Breakfast Bagels

Serves: 4

Prep time: 10 mins / Cook time: 15 mins

Ingredients:
- 125 g self raising flour
- 1 egg
- 245 g fat free greek yogurt

Preparation Procedures::
1. Mix together the Greek yogurt and self-raising flour.
2. Lightly flour a flat surface for kneading.
3. Knead the dough for about 5 minutes.
4. Divide the dough into 4 pieces.
5. Roll each piece into a long rope and form into a bagel shape.
6. Beat egg.
7. Brush each bagel with egg wash.
8. Place each bagel in an air fryer basket.
9. Cook for 15 minutes at 180°C

Breakfast Hash

Serves: 2

Prep time: 10 mins / Cook time: 25 mins

Ingredients:
- 450 g baby potatoes
- 40 g chopped onion
- 1 tsp paprika
- ½ tsp cumin
- ½ tsp turmeric
- ½ red pepper (finely chopped)
- ½ tsp garlic powder
- 2 tbsp olive oil

Preparation Procedures:
1. Dice potatoes into small cubes.
2. Mix potatoes, onion, peppers, spices and oil together in a bowl.
3. Preheat air fryer at 180°C.
4. Put potato mixture in air fryer and cook for 10 minutes.
5. Shake basket after 10 minutes.
6. Cook for an additional 15 minutes.
7. Serve with a poached egg on top.

Avocado Egg Boats with Sausages

Serves 4

Prep time: 10 minutes / Cook time: 10 minutes

Ingredients:
- 2 large avocados
- 4 small eggs
- 1 tsp olive oil
- Sea salt and ground black pepper, to taste
- 4 small pork sausages, casing removed

Preparation Procedures:
1. Insert crisper plates in both drawers. Spray the plates with nonstick cooking oil.
2. Cut the avocado into halves and remove the stone. Scoop out some inner flesh using a spoon.
3. Crack an egg into each avocado half. Brush them with olive oil and season with salt and black pepper.
4. Prick the sausages with a fork several times.
5. Add avocado halves to the zone 1 drawer; add the sausages to the zone 2 drawer.
6. Select zone 1 and pair it with "BAKE" at 190°C for 10 minutes. Select zone 2 and pair it with "AIR FRY" at 180°C for 9 minutes
7. Select "SYNC" followed by the "START/STOP" button. At the halfway point, shake your food or toss it with silicone-tipped tongs to promote even cooking.

Herb Butter Rolls

Prep time: 4-5 hours
Cook time: 12-13 minutes
Serves 6

Ingredients:
- 1 tsp olive oil
- 6 frozen dinner rolls, thawed
- 2 tbsp butter, melted
- 1 tbsp dried rosemary
- 1 tbsp dried thyme
- 1 tsp dried oregano
- 1/4 tsp salt
- 1/4 tsp ground black pepper

Preparation Procedures:
1. Remove a crisper plate from your Nina Foodi. Brush the inside of two small baking tins with olive oil.
2. Divide the rolls between baking tins. Place in a warm space for 4 to 5 hours, until the rolls double in size.
3. In the meantime, preheat your Ninja Foodi to 165°C for about 5 minutes.
4. Melt butter, along with the herbs, salt, and black pepper in a small dish. Brush the herb butter on top of defrosted rolls; put the pans into the drawers.
5. Select zone 1 and pair it with "BAKE" at 165°C for 12 to 13 minutes. Select "MATCH" followed by the "START/STOP" button.
6. Check the loaves for doneness and let them sit on a cooling rack for about 10 minutes before cutting and serving. Bon appétit!

Star Anise Muffins

Serves 8
Prep time: 10 minutes / Cook time: 15 minutes

Ingredients:
- 2 large eggs
- 300g apple sauce
- 200g brown sugar
- 100g coconut oil
- 200g self-raising plain flour
- A pinch of sea salt
- 1/4 tsp ground anise
- 1/4 tsp ground cinnamon

Preparation Procedures:
1. Remove a crisper plate from your Ninja Foodi. Preheat the Ninja Foodi to 160°C for 5 minutes. Spray 8 muffin cases with nonstick oil.
2. In a separate mixing bowl, whisk the eggs until pale and frothy. Slowly and gradually, stir in apple sauce, brown sugar, and coconut oil; mix until everything is well incorporated.
3. In another bowl, thoroughly combine the dry ingredients.
4. Slowly and gradually, add the dry Ingredients to the wet ingredients; mix again to combine. Spoon the batter into the prepared muffin cases. Place 4 muffin cases in each drawer.
5. Select zone 1 and pair it with "BAKE" at 160°C for 15 minutes. Select "MATCH" followed by the "START/STOP" button.
6. Allow your muffins to rest on a cooling rack for about 10 minutes before unmolding and serving.

Baked Eggs with Vegetables

Serves 6
Prep time: 10 minutes / Cook time: 12 minutes

Ingredients:
- 100g double cream
- 2 medium bell peppers, seeded and chopped
- 2 large tomatoes, chopped
- 300ml canned full-fat coconut milk
- 400g spinach
- 1/2 tsp chilli flakes
- 6 whole eggs
- Sea salt and ground black pepper, to taste

Preparation Procedures:
1. Remove a crisper plate from your Nina Foodi. Preheat the Ninja Foodi to 180°C for 5 minutes.
2. Add the double cream, peppers, tomatoes, milk, spinach, and chilli flakes to a mixing bowl.
3. Divide the mixture between two baking tins; add the tins to the air fryer drawers. Make three holes in each mixture with the back of a tablespoon; now, crack an egg into each hole.
4. Sprinkle the eggs with salt and black pepper.
5. Select zone 1 and pair it with "BAKE" at 180°C

for 12 minutes. Select "MATCH" followed by the "START/STOP" button.

Breakfast Bars

Serves 12
Prep time: 5 minutes /Cook time: 15 minutes

Ingredients:

- 60g raisins
- 20g sunflower seed
- 20g pumpkin seeds
- 150g oats
- 30g multigrain hoop cereal
- 100g coconut oil, softened
- 100g brown sugar
- 100g honey

Preparation Procedures:

1. Begin by preheating your Ninja Foodi to 180°C.
2. In a mixing bowl, thoroughly combine all Ingredients until everything is well combined.
3. Spoon the mixture into two parchment-lined roasting tins; press down the mixture with a wide spatula. Place the baking tins in both drawers.
4. Select zone 1 and pair it with "BAKE" at 180°C for 15 minutes. Select "MATCH" followed by the "START/STOP" button.
5. Let it cool before slicing it into bars.

Breakfast Crunchy Cereals

Serves 7
Prep time: 5 minutes / Cook time: 15 minutes

Ingredients:

- 200g rolled oats
- 100g pumpkin seeds
- 100g peanut butter
- 30g hemp seeds
- 60g almonds, slivered
- 100g agave syrup
- 1/2 tsp ground cloves
- 1/2 tsp ground cinnamon
- 30g sesame seeds

Preparation Procedures:

1. Begin by preheating your Ninja Foodi to 170°C.
2. In a mixing bowl, thoroughly combine rolled oats, pumpkin seeds, peanut butter, hemp seeds, almonds, agave syrup, ground cloves, and cinnamon.
3. Spoon the mixture into two parchment-lined roasting tins; press down slightly using a silicone spatula. Place the baking tins in both drawers.
4. Select zone 1 and pair it with "BAKE" at 170°C for 15 minutes. Select "MATCH" followed by the "START/STOP" button.
5. When zone 1 time reaches 8 minutes, add sesame seeds, and reinsert the drawer to continue cooking.
6. Let your cereals cool before serving and storing. Enjoy!

Chapter 2: Beans and Grains Recipes

Crispy Chickpea Snack

Servings: 2
Prep time: 6 minutes / Cook time: 20 minutes

Ingredients:
- 1 can (425g) chickpeas, drained and rinsed
- 1 tablespoon olive oil
- 1 teaspoon ground cumin
- 1 teaspoon smoked paprika
- 1/2 teaspoon garlic powder
- Salt to taste

Preparation Instructions:
1. Preheat your Ninja Dual Zone Air Fryer to 200°C.
2. Combine chickpeas, olive oil, cumin, smoked paprika, garlic powder, and salt in a mixing bowl. Toss the mixture thoroughly to coat the chickpeas evenly.
3. Place the seasoned chickpeas in the air fryer drawer in a single layer.
4. Cook for 15-20 minutes, shaking the drawer halfway through, until the chickpeas are crispy and golden brown.
5. Remove the chickpeas from the air fryer and let them cool slightly before serving.

Black Bean Tacos with Avocado Crema

Servings: 2
Prep time: 10 minutes / Cook time: 6 minutes

Ingredients:
For the tacos:
- 1 can (425g) black beans, drained and rinsed
- 1 teaspoon olive oil
- 1 small onion, finely chopped
- 2 cloves garlic, minced
- 1 teaspoon ground cumin
- 1 teaspoon chili powder
- Salt and pepper to taste
- Tortillas (corn or flour)

For the avocado crema:
- 1 ripe avocado
- 20ml plain Greek yogurt
- 1 tablespoon lime juice
- Salt to taste

Preparation Instructions:
1. Preheat your Ninja Dual Zone Air Fryer to 200°C.
2. In a skillet over medium heat, warm the olive oil. Add the chopped onion, minced garlic, and sauté until the onion becomes translucent.
3. Add the skillet's black beans, cumin, chili powder, salt, and pepper. Stir well to combine, and cook for 3-4 minutes until the beans are heated.
4. Meanwhile, prepare the avocado crema by blending the avocado, Greek yogurt, lime juice, and salt in a food processor or blender until smooth and creamy. Set this aside.
5. Warm your tortillas in the air fryer for a few seconds until they are pliable.
6. To assemble the tacos, spoon the black bean mixture onto the tortillas and top using your selected toppings. Drizzle the avocado crema over the tacos.
7. Serve immediately and enjoy the flavorful black bean tacos with avocado crema.

Quinoa Stuffed Bell Peppers

Servings: 2
Prep time: 10 minutes / Cook time: 23 minutes

Ingredients:
- 4 bell peppers (any color)
- 240ml cooked quinoa
- 1 can (425g) black beans, drained and rinsed
- 240g diced tomatoes
- 80g corn kernels (fresh or frozen)
- 60g shredded cheddar cheese (or cheese of your choice)
- 1 teaspoon cumin
- 1 teaspoon chili powder
- Salt and pepper to taste
- Fresh cilantro for garnish (optional)

Preparation Instructions:

1. Preheat your Ninja Dual Zone Air Fryer to 190°C.
2. Cut the tops off the bell peppers and remove the seeds and membranes.
3. Combine the cooked quinoa, black beans, diced tomatoes, corn kernels, cumin, chili powder, salt, and pepper in a mixing bowl. Mix it vigorously and thoroughly.
4. Stuff each bell pepper with the quinoa mixture, packing it tightly. Place the stuffed peppers in the air fryer drawer.
5. Cook the stuffed peppers in the air fryer for 18-20 minutes, or until the peppers are tender and the filling is heated through.
6. Sprinkle the shredded cheese over the tops of the peppers and return them to the air fryer for another 2-3 minutes, or until the cheese is melted and bubbly.
7. Carefully remove the stuffed peppers from the air fryer and let them cool for a few minutes.
8. Garnish with fresh cilantro and serve hot.

Air Fryer Lentil Burgers

Servings: 2

Prep time: 5 minutes / Cook time: 12 minutes

Ingredients:

- 200g cooked lentils
- 60g breadcrumbs
- 30g finely chopped onion
- 2 cloves garlic, minced
- 1 tablespoon soy sauce
- 1 teaspoon ground cumin
- 1/2 teaspoon paprika
- Salt and pepper to taste
- Burger buns

Preparation Instructions:

1. Preheat your Ninja Dual Zone Air Fryer to 190°C.
2. In a mixing bowl, mash the cooked lentils using a fork or air fryerato masher.
3. Add the breadcrumbs, chopped onion, minced garlic, soy sauce, cumin, paprika, salt, and pepper to the bowl. Mix well to combine all the ingredients.

4. Shape the lentil mixture into patties of your desired size.
5. Place the lentil patties in the air fryer drawer, ensuring they are not touching each other.
6. Cook the lentil burgers in the air fryer for 10-12 minutes, flipping them halfway through, until they are crispy and golden brown.
7. Remove the lentil burgers from the air fryer and let them cool slightly.
8. Serve the lentil burgers on burger buns with any desired toppings, such as lettuce, tomato, onion, and condiments.

Mexican Rice and Beans

Servings: 2

Prep time: 5 minutes / Cook time: 18 minutes

Ingredients:

- 185g long-grain rice
- 1 tablespoon olive oil
- 80g Diced onion
- 75g diced bell pepper
- 2 cloves garlic, minced
- 1 can (425g) of black beans, drained and rinsed
- 1 can (411g) of diced tomatoes
- 1 teaspoon chili powder
- 1/2 teaspoon ground cumin
- Salt and pepper to taste
- Fresh cilantro for garnish

Preparation Instructions:

1. Preheat your Ninja Dual Zone Air Fryer to 182°C.
2. In a skillet over medium heat, heat the olive oil. Add the diced onion, bell pepper, and minced garlic. Sauté until the vegetables become tender.
3. Add the rice to the skillet and cook, stirring frequently, for 2-3 minutes until the rice grains are coated with oil and lightly toasted.
4. Transfer the rice mixture to the air fryer drawer. Add the black beans, diced tomatoes, chili powder, cumin, salt, and pepper. Stir well to combine.
5. Set Zone 1 to "AIR FRY" and put the rice mixture in.
6. Cook the rice and beans in the air fryer for 15-18 minutes, stirring halfway through, until the rice

is cooked and fluffy.

7. Once cooked, garnish with fresh cilantro, if desired, and serve hot.

Cajun Spiced Pinto Beans

Servings: 2
Prep time: 4 minutes / Cook time: 12 minutes

Ingredients:
- 2 cans of pinto beans, drained and rinsed
- 1 tablespoon olive oil
- 80g diced onion
- 75g diced bell pepper
- 2 cloves garlic, minced
- 1 teaspoon Cajun seasoning
- 1/2 teaspoon smoked paprika
- Salt and pepper to taste
- Chopped green onions

Preparation Instructions:
1. Preheat your Ninja Dual Zone Air Fryer to 193°C.
2. In a skillet over medium heat, warm the olive oil. Add the diced onion, bell pepper, and minced garlic. Sauté until the vegetables become tender.
3. Add the drained and rinsed pinto beans to the skillet. Stir in the Cajun seasoning, smoked paprika, salt, and pepper. Mix well to coat the beans with the spices.
4. Transfer the seasoned pinto beans to the air fryer drawer and spread them out in a single layer.
5. Cook the pinto beans in the air fryer for 10-12 minutes, shaking the drawer occasionally, until the beans are heated and slightly crispy.
6. Remove the Cajun spiced pinto beans from the air fryer and let them cool for a few minutes.
7. Garnish with chopped green onions, if desired, and serve as a flavorful side dish or a filling for your tacos, burritos, or bowls.

Air Fried Falafel

Servings: 2
Prep time: 5 minutes / Cook time: 15 minutes

Ingredients:
- 237g dried chickpeas
- 1 small onion, roughly chopped
- 3 cloves garlic
- 15g fresh parsley leaves
- 4g fresh cilantro leaves
- 1 teaspoon ground cumin
- 1 teaspoon ground coriander
- 1/2 teaspoon baking soda
- 1 tablespoon lemon juice
- Salt to taste
- 2 tablespoons olive oil (for brushing)

Preparation Instructions:
1. Soak the dried chickpeas in water overnight. Drain and rinse them thoroughly.
2. Combine the soaked chickpeas, onion, garlic, parsley, cilantro, cumin, coriander, baking soda, lemon juice, and salt in a food processor. Pulse until all the Ingredients are well combined and the mixture forms a coarse paste.
3. Shape the falafel mixture into small patties or balls, about 1-2 inches in diameter.
4. Preheat your Ninja Dual Zone Air Fryer to 200°C for 5 minutes.
5. Lightly brush the falafel patties with olive oil on both sides.
6. Place the falafel patties in the air fryer drawer, ensuring they are not touching each other.
7. Cook the falafel in the air fryer for 12-15 minutes, flipping them halfway through the cooking time until golden brown and crispy.
8. Once cooked, remove the falafel from the air fryer and serve them hot with pita bread, tahini sauce, and your favorite salad ingredients.

Garlic Butter Rice with Black Beans

Servings: 2

Prep time: / Cook time: 12 minutes

Ingredients:

- 185g long-grain white rice
- 473ml vegetable or chicken broth
- 2 tablespoons butter
- 3 cloves garlic, minced
- 1 can (425g) black beans, drained and rinsed
- Salt and pepper to taste
- Chopped fresh parsley (optional, for garnish)

Preparation Instructions:

1. Rinse the rice under cold water until the water runs clear. Drain well.
2. In the inner air pot of your Ninja Dual Zone Air Fryer, melt the butter using the "REHEAT" function.
3. Add the minced garlic to the melted butter and sauté for about 1 minute until fragrant.
4. Add the rice to the air fryer and stir well to coat it with the garlic butter.
5. Pour in the vegetable or chicken broth and season with salt and pepper.
6. Close the lid and cook the rice using the "AIR FRY"ing function (typically around 10-12 minutes for white rice).
7. Once the rice is cooked, let it sit for a few minutes before carefully releasing any remaining pressure.
8. Open the lid and fluff the rice with a fork. Stir in the black beans.
9. Close the lid and let the rice and beans sit in the air fryer for a few more minutes to warm the beans.
10. Serve the garlic butter rice with black beans hot, garnished with chopped fresh parsley if desired.

Crispy Parmesan Quinoa Bites

Servings: 2

Prep time: 10 minutes / Cook time: 12 minutes

Ingredients:

- 185g cooked quinoa
- 50g grated Parmesan cheese
- 25g breadcrumbs
- 2 green onions, finely chopped
- 1 egg, lightly beaten
- 1/2 teaspoon garlic powder
- Salt and pepper to taste
- Olive oil spray

Preparation Instructions:

1. Combine the cooked quinoa, grated Parmesan cheese, breadcrumbs, green onions, egg, garlic powder, salt, and pepper in a mixing bowl.
2. Stir the mixture well until all the Ingredients are evenly combined.
3. Preheat your Ninja Dual Zone Air Fryer to (200°C) for 5 minutes.
4. Shape the quinoa mixture into small bite-sized balls or patties using your hands.
5. Place the quinoa bites on a baking sheet lined with parchment paper.
6. Lightly spray the quinoa bites with olive oil to promote crispiness.
7. Transfer the quinoa bites to the air fryer drawer, ensuring they do not touch each other.
8. Air fry the quinoa bites at 200°C for 10-12 minutes, or until they turn golden brown and crispy.
9. Once cooked, remove the quinoa bites from the air fryer and let them cool slightly before serving.
10. Serve the crispy Parmesan quinoa bites as an appetizer, or a nice mid-day snack.

Southwest Quinoa Salad

Servings: 2
Prep time: / Cook time:

Ingredients:
- 185g quinoa
- 470ml vegetable broth
- 1 can (425g) black beans, rinsed and drained
- 160g corn kernels
- 1 red bell pepper, diced
- 1/2 red onion, diced
- 1 jalapeno, seeded and minced
- 4g fresh cilantro, chopped
- Juice of 1 lime
- 2 tablespoons olive oil
- 1 teaspoon ground cumin
- Salt and pepper to taste
- Optional toppings: avocado, cherry tomatoes, feta cheese

Preparation Instructions:
1. Rinse the quinoa thoroughly under cold water and drain.
2. Combine the rinsed quinoa and vegetable broth in the Ninja Dual Zone Air Fryer air fryer.
3. Close the lid and set the air fryer to "AIR FRY" on high for 1 minute. Once done, release the pressure manually and remove the quinoa from the air fryer.
4. Combine the cooked quinoa, black beans, corn, red bell pepper, red onion, jalapeno, and cilantro in a large bowl.
5. Whisk together the lime juice, olive oil, cumin, salt, and pepper in a separate small bowl.
6. Pour the dressing over the quinoa mixture and toss until well combined.
7. If desired, serve the Southwest quinoa salad as is or garnish with avocado, cherry tomatoes, and feta cheese.

Cajun Black Eyed Peas

Servings: 2
Prep time: / Cook time:

Ingredients:
- 400g dried black-eyed peas
- 940ml vegetable broth
- 1 onion, diced
- 2 cloves garlic, minced
- 1 green bell pepper, diced
- 1 stalk celery, diced
- 1 can diced tomatoes
- 2 teaspoons Cajun seasoning
- 1 teaspoon smoked paprika
- 1/2 teaspoon dried thyme
- Salt and pepper to taste
- Chopped green onions for garnish (optional)

Preparation Instructions:
1. Rinse the dried black-eyed peas under cold water and drain.
2. In the Ninja Dual Zone Air Fryer air fryer, combine the black-eyed peas, vegetable broth, onion, garlic, green bell pepper, celery, diced tomatoes (with their juice), Cajun seasoning, smoked paprika, dried thyme, salt, and pepper.
3. Close the lid and set the air fryer to "AIR FRY" on high for 15 minutes. Once done, allow the pressure to release naturally for 10 minutes before manually releasing any remaining pressure.
4. Open the lid and stir the black-eyed peas. If the mixture seems too liquidy, you can use the air frying function to reduce the liquid. Close the lid and select the air fryer function at 375°F (190°C) for 5-10 minutes, stirring occasionally, until desired consistency is reached.
5. Taste and adjust the seasoning if needed.
6. If desired, serve the Cajun black-eyed peas hot, garnished with chopped green onions.

Air Fryer Refried Beans

Servings: 2
Prep time: / Cook time:

Ingredients:
- 2 cans (425g each) pinto beans, drained and rinsed
- 1 tablespoon olive oil
- 1/2 onion, diced
- 2 cloves garlic, minced
- 1 teaspoon ground cumin
- 1/2 teaspoon chili powder
- 1/4 teaspoon smoked paprika
- Salt and pepper to taste

Preparation Instructions:
1. Add olive oil and diced onion to the Air Fryer. Select the sauté function and cook for a few minutes until the onion becomes translucent.
2. Add the minced garlic and sauté for another minute.
3. Add the drained and rinsed pinto beans to the air fryer, ground cumin, chili powder, smoked paprika, salt, and pepper. Stir well to combine.
4. Close the lid of the Air Fryer and select the air fryer function at 375°F (190°C). Cook for 10-12 minutes, stirring occasionally, until the beans are heated through and start to brown slightly.
5. Once cooked, remove the air fryer from the air fryer and allow the beans to cool slightly.
6. Using a air fryerato masher or fork, mash the beans until they reach your desired consistency. You can add a splash of water or vegetable broth to achieve the desired texture if needed.
7. Taste and adjust the seasoning if needed.
8. Serve the air fryer refried beans as a side dish or use them in your favorite Mexican-inspired recipes like burritos, tacos, or enchiladas.

Spicy Chickpea Curry

Servings: 2
Prep time: / Cook time:

Ingredients:
- 2 cans chickpeas (425g each), drained and rinsed
- 1 onion, finely chopped
- 2 cloves garlic, minced
- 1 tablespoon ginger, grated
- 1 can (411g) diced tomatoes
- 1 can (400ml) coconut milk
- 2 tablespoons curry powder
- 1 teaspoon ground cumin
- 1/2 teaspoon turmeric
- 1/2 teaspoon paprika
- 1/4 teaspoon cayenne pepper (adjust to taste)
- Salt and pepper to taste
- Fresh cilantro for garnish

Preparation Instructions:
1. Preheat the Ninja Dual Zone Air Fryer using the Saute function.
2. Add the chopped onion, minced garlic, and grated ginger to the air fryer and sauté until the onion becomes translucent.
3. Add the curry powder, ground cumin, turmeric, paprika, and cayenne pepper to the air fryer. Stir well to coat the onion mixture with the spices.
4. Pour in the diced tomatoes (with their juice) and coconut milk. Stir to combine.
5. Add the drained chickpeas to the air fryer and season with salt and pepper. Stir again.
6. Close the lid and select the "AIR FRY" function. Set the timer for 5 minutes.
7. Once the cooking time is complete, allow the pressure to release naturally for 5 minutes before manually releasing any remaining pressure.
8. Open the lid and stir the chickpea curry. Taste and adjust the seasoning if needed.
9. Serve the spicy chickpea curry hot, garnished with fresh cilantro. It pairs well with steamed rice or naan bread.

Herbed Farro Pilaf

Servings: 2
Prep time: / Cook time:

Ingredients:
- 240ml farro
- 480ml vegetable broth
- 1 tablespoon olive oil
- 1 onion, diced
- 2 cloves garlic, minced
- 1 teaspoon dried thyme
- 1 teaspoon dried rosemary

- Salt and pepper to taste

Preparation Instructions:

1. Rinse the farro under cold water and drain.
2. Heat the olive oil using the Saute function in the Ninja Dual Zone Air Fryer air fryer.
3. Add the diced onion and minced garlic to the air fryer and sauté until the onion becomes translucent.
4. Add the rinsed farro, dried thyme, rosemary, salt, and pepper to the air fryer. Stir well to coat the farro with the onion mixture and herbs.
5. Pour in the vegetable broth and give it a quick stir.
6. Close the lid and select the "AIR FRY" function. Set the timer for 15 minutes.
7. Once the cooking time is complete, allow the pressure to release naturally for 10 minutes before manually releasing any remaining pressure.
8. Open the lid and fluff the farro pilaf with a fork. Taste and adjust the seasoning if needed.
9. Serve the herbed farro pilaf hot, garnished with chopped parsley if desired. It makes a delicious side dish for roasted vegetables or grilled meats.

Sweet air fryerato and Black Bean Enchiladas

Servings: 2
Prep time: / Cook time:

Ingredients:
- 2 medium sweet air fryeratoes, peeled and diced
- 1 can (425g) black beans, drained and rinsed
- 1 onion, diced
- 2 cloves garlic, minced
- 1 teaspoon ground cumin
- 1/2 teaspoon chili powder
- Salt and pepper to taste
- 8 small corn tortillas
- 240ml enchilada sauce
- Shredded cheese

Preparation Instructions:

1. Preheat the Air Fryer using the Bake/Roast function at (200°C).
2. Combine the diced sweet air fryeratoes, black

beans, diced onion, minced garlic, ground cumin, chili powder, salt, and pepper in a mixing bowl. Toss until the Ingredients are well mixed.

3. Spread the sweet air fryerato and black bean mixture on the Air Fryer Sheet Pan in one of the cooking zones.
4. Place the sheet pan in the Air Fryer and bake for about 20-25 minutes or until the sweet air fryeratoes are tender and slightly crispy, stirring halfway through.
5. While the sweet air fryerato and black bean mixture is baking, warm the corn tortillas in a microwave or skillet.
6. Remove the sheet pan from the Air Fryer and transfer the cooked sweet air fryerato and black bean mixture to a bowl.
7. Pour half of the enchilada sauce in the other cooking zone of the Ninja Dual Zone Air Fryer.
8. Dip each warmed tortilla into the enchilada sauce, coating both sides.
9. Fill each tortilla with a spoonful of the sweet air fryerato and black bean mixture and roll it tightly. Place the enchiladas seam-side down in the Air Fryer, on top of the sauce.
10. Pour the remaining enchilada sauce over the enchiladas and sprinkle shredded cheese.
11. Close the lid and select the Bake/Roast function at 375°F (190°C). Cook for 10-12 minutes or until the cheese is melted and bubbly.
12. Once cooked, remove the enchiladas from the Air Fryer, garnish with chopped cilantro

Air Fried Rice and Lentils

Servings: 2
Prep time: 3 minutes / Cook time: 12 minutes

Ingredients:
- 185g cooked rice
- 200g cooked lentils
- 1 tablespoon vegetable oil
- 1/2 onion, diced
- 1 carrot, diced
- 50g frozen peas
- 2 cloves garlic, minced
- 2 tablespoons soy sauce
- 1 tablespoon sesame oil

- Salt and pepper to taste
- Optional toppings: chopped green onions, sesame seeds

Preparation Instructions:
1. Preheat the Ninja Dual Zone Air Fryer using the "Bake/Roast" function at 200°C.
2. Add vegetable oil and diced onion to one of the cooking zones. Cook for a few minutes until the onion becomes translucent.
3. Add the diced carrot, frozen peas, and minced garlic to the Air Fryer. Cook for another 2-3 minutes, stirring occasionally.
4. In the other cooking zone, add the cooked rice and cooked lentils. Break up any clumps and spread them evenly.
5. Place the vegetables and the rice-lentil mixture in the Ninja Dual Zone Air Fryer and bake for about 10-12 minutes, stirring halfway through, or until the rice and lentils are heated through and slightly crispy.
6. Remove both zones from the Air Fryer and combine the cooked vegetables with the rice and lentils in a bowl.
7. Drizzle soy sauce and sesame oil over the mixture. Season with salt and pepper to taste. Toss everything together until well coated and serve.

Mediterranean Couscous Salad

Servings: 2
Prep time: 3 minutes / Cook time: 5 minutes

Ingredients:
- 173g couscous
- 230ml vegetable broth
- 1 cucumber, diced
- 1 tomato, diced
- 1/2 red onion, diced
- 50g Kalamata olives, sliced
- 28g feta cheese, crumbled
- 2 tablespoons fresh lemon juice
- 2 tablespoons olive oil
- 1 tablespoon chopped fresh parsley
- Salt and pepper to taste

Preparation Instructions:

1. Combine the couscous and vegetable broth in the Ninja Dual Zone Air Fryer.
2. Close the lid and set the air fryer to "AIR FRY" on high for 2 minutes. Once done, allow the pressure to release naturally for 5 minutes before manually releasing any remaining pressure.
3. Open the lid and fluff the cooked couscous with a fork. Allow it to cool slightly.
4. In a large bowl, combine the cooled couscous, diced cucumber, tomato, red onion, sliced Kalamata olives, and crumbled feta cheese.
5. Whisk together the fresh lemon juice, olive oil, chopped parsley, salt, and pepper in a small bowl.
6. Pour the dressing over the couscous salad and toss until the salad and dressing are well combined.
7. Taste and adjust the seasoning if needed.
8. Serve the Mediterranean couscous salad chilled.

Mexican Style Air Fryer Rice

Servings: 2
Prep time: 4 minutes / Cook time: 8 minutes

Ingredients:
- 185g long-grain white rice
- 355ml vegetable broth
- 1 tablespoon vegetable oil
- 1/2 onion, diced
- 1 jalapeno, seeded and minced
- 1 clove garlic, minced
- 1 teaspoon ground cumin
- 1 teaspoon chili powder
- 1/2 teaspoon salt
- 1 can diced tomatoes, drained
- Freshly chopped fresh cilantro
- Juice of 1 lime

Preparation Instructions:
1. Measure and rinse out the white rice under cold water and drain.
2. Heat the vegetable oil using the Saute function in the Ninja Food Dual Zone Air Fryer.
3. Add the diced onion and minced jalapeno to the air fryer. Cook for a few minutes until the onion becomes translucent.
4. Add the minced garlic, ground cumin, chili

powder, and salt to the air fryer. Stir well to coat the onion mixture with the spices.

5. Add the rinsed rice to the air fryer and stir to combine with the onion and spice mixture.

6. Pour in the vegetable broth and drained diced tomatoes. Stir again.

7. Close the lid and select the "AIR FRY" function. Set the timer for 3 minutes.

8. Once the cooking time is complete, allow the pressure to release naturally for 5 minutes before manually releasing any remaining pressure.

9. Open the lid and give the rice a gentle stir. It should be cooked and tender.

10. Add the chopped fresh cilantro and squeeze the lime juice over the rice. Stir to incorporate the flavors.

11. Serve the Mexican-style air fryer rice hot as a side dish or base for your favorite Mexican-inspired dishes.

Quinoa and Black Bean Stuffed Zucchini Boats

Servings: 2
Prep time: 9 minutes / Cook time: 23 minutes

Ingredients:
- 4 medium zucchini
- Cooked quinoa
- 1 can (425g) black beans, drained and rinsed
- 1/2 red bell pepper, diced
- 1/2 yellow bell pepper, diced
- 1/2 onion, diced
- 2 cloves garlic, minced
- 1 teaspoon ground cumin
- 1/2 teaspoon chili powder
- Salt and pepper to taste
- 20g shredded cheese (such as cheddar or Monterey Jack)
- Chopped fresh cilantro

Preparation Instructions:
1. Preheat the Ninja Dual Zone Air Fryer using the Bake/Roast function at 190°C.
2. Cut each zucchini in half lengthwise, creating boat-shaped halves. Scoop out the flesh from the center of each zucchini half, leaving a hollow space for the filling. Set the hollowed zucchini

aside.

3. In a mixing bowl, combine the cooked quinoa, black beans, red bell pepper, yellow bell pepper, diced onion, minced garlic, ground cumin, chili powder, salt, and pepper. Stir well to mix all the ingredients.

4. Fill each hollowed zucchini boat with the quinoa and black bean mixture. Press the filling down gently to pack it in.

5. Place the stuffed zucchini in one of the cooking zones of the Ninja Dual Zone Air Fryer and bake for about 20-25 minutes or until the zucchini is tender and the filling is heated through.

6. Sprinkle the shredded cheese in the other cooking zone on each stuffed zucchini boat. Continue baking for 2-3 minutes or until the cheese is melted and bubbly.

7. Carefully remove the zucchini boats from the Air Fryer and garnish with chopped fresh cilantro.

8. Serve the quinoa and black bean stuffed zucchini boats as a flavorful and nutritious main dish. Enjoy!

Barbecue Baked Beans

Servings: 2
Prep time: 7 minutes / Cook time: 15 minutes

Ingredients:
- 2 cans (425g) of navy beans, drained and rinsed
- 1/2 onion, diced
- 2 cloves garlic, minced
- 120ml Barbecue sauce
- 2 tablespoons tomato paste
- 2 tablespoons brown sugar
- 1 tablespoon Dijon mustard
- 1 tablespoon apple cider vinegar
- 1/2 teaspoon smoked paprika
- Salt and pepper to taste
- Sliced green onions for toppings.

Preparation Instructions:
1. Preheat the Ninja Dual Zone Air Fryer using the Saute function.
2. Add the diced onion and minced garlic to the air fryer and sauté until the onion becomes translucent.
3. Add the drained navy beans to the air fryer and

stir to combine with the onion and garlic.

4. Whisk together the barbecue sauce, tomato paste, brown sugar, Dijon mustard, apple cider vinegar, smoked paprika, salt, and pepper in a small bowl.

5. Pour the barbecue sauce mixture over the beans and stir well to coat.

6. Close the lid of the Ninja Dual Zone Air Fryer and select the "AIR FRY" function. Set the timer for 10 minutes.

7. Once the cooking time is complete, allow the pressure to release naturally for 5 minutes before manually releasing any remaining pressure.

8. Open the lid and give the baked beans a stir. Taste and adjust the seasoning if needed.

9. Serve the barbecue baked beans hot, garnished with sliced green onions.

Baked Beans with Sausages

Serves 5

Prep time: 10 minutes / Cook time: 20 minutes

Ingredients:

- 1 tsp olive oil
- 2 (400g) cans Pinto beans, drained
- 1 red bell pepper, seeded and chopped
- 1 large onion, chopped
- 2 garlic cloves, minced
- 500g passata
- 2 tsp bouillon powder
- 1/4 tsp cumin seeds, ground
- 1/4 tsp coriander seeds, ground
- 1 bay leaf
- 5 whole Italian sausages

Preparation Instructions:

1. Brush the inside of an oven-safe baking tin with olive oil. Add the beans, pepper, onions, garlic, passata, bouillon powder, cumin, coriander, and bay leaf.

2. Place the baking tin in the zone 1 drawer. Place the sausages in the zone 2 drawer.

3. Select zone 1 and pair it with "BAKE" at 180°C for 20 minutes. Select zone 2 and pair it with "AIRFRY" at 200°C for 16 minutes. Select "SYNC" followed by the "START/STOP" button.

4. When zone 1 time reaches 10 minutes, stir the beans, and reinsert the drawers to continue cooking.

5. When zone 2 time reaches 8 minutes, flip the sausages over to ensure even browning; reinsert drawers to continue cooking.

6. Bon appétit!

Roasted Garbanzo Bean and Pepper Salad

Serves 4

Prep time: 10 minutes / Cook time: 15 minutes

Ingredients:

- 500g garbanzo beans, drained and rinsed
- 1 tbsp olive oil
- Sea salt and ground black pepper, to taste
- 1/2 tsp garlic granules
- 1/2 tsp onion granules
- 1 tsp hot paprika
- 4 bell peppers, seeded
- 1 fresh garlic clove, minced
- 2 tbsp fresh parsley leaves, chopped
- 1 tbsp extra-virgin olive oil
- 2 tbsp apple cider vinegar

Preparation Instructions:

1. Toss the garbanzo beans with 1 tablespoon of olive oil, salt, black pepper, garlic, onion granules, and paprika.

2. Place the garbanzo beans in the zone 1 drawer. Place the peppers in the zone 2 drawer and spray them with nonstick cooking oil.

3. Select zone 1 and pair it with "ROAST" at 200°C for 15 minutes. Select "MATCH" to duplicate settings across both zones. Press the "START/STOP" button.

4. When zone 1 time reaches 8 minutes, shake the drawers to ensure even browning; reinsert the drawers to continue cooking.

5. Cut the roasted peppers into slices. Toss roasted garbanzo beans and peppers in a salad bowl; add the other Ingredients and toss to combine well. Enjoy!

Rustic Porridge Bread

Serves 4

Prep time: 1 hour 45 minutes / Cook time: 30 minutes

Ingredients:
- 200g leftover oatmeal, room temperature
- 300ml lukewarm water
- 500g plain flour
- 2 tbsp honey
- A pinch of sea salt
- A pinch of ground cloves
- 1 tsp ground cinnamon
- 8g dried yeast

Preparation Instructions:
1. Add leftover porridge and water to a large mixing bowl. Add the other Ingredients and stir until everything is well combined.
2. Cover the bowl with a tea towel and leave it to prove in a warm place for approximately 1 hour, until it has doubled in size.
3. Knead the dough on a lightly floured surface and divide it into two loaves; place the loaves in two lightly buttered loaf tins. Let them stand for another 40 minutes.
4. Meanwhile, preheat your Ninja Foodi to 165°C for about 5 minutes.
5. Brush the loaves with nonstick cooking oil. Add the loaf tins to your Ninja Foodi.
6. Select zone 1 and pair it with "BAKE" at 165°C for 30 minutes. Select "MATCH" followed by the "START/STOP" button.
7. Check the loaves for doneness and let them sit on a cooling rack for about 10 minutes before cutting and serving. Devour!

Bean Bakes

Serves 4

Prep time: 1 minutes | Cook time: 15 minutes

Ingredients:
- 4 bean bakes, frozen
- 1cal olive fry spray

Preparation Instructions:
1. Remove the bean bakes from packet and place 2 in each zone of the dual zone, then spray them thoroughly
2. Pair the zones with 'BAKE' at 180°C for 15 minutes
3. Press 'MATCH' then 'START/STOP' to start baking the content
4. At the half way point, flip the bean bakes and spray them again
5. Once cooked, retrieve the bean bakes to serve

Crispy Cannellini Beans

Serves 6

Prep time: 5 minutes | Cook time: 15 minutes

Ingredients:
- 420g cannellini beans, dried
- 1 tsp Italian seasoning Mix
- 1 tbsp flaxseed oil

Preparation Instructions:
1. Preheat the dual zone to 200°C for 3 minutes
2. Meanwhile, add the beans into a large mixing bowl, then add oil and Italian seasoning
3. Toss the beans in both draws of the dual zone and pair them to 'BAKE' at 200°C for 15 minutes
4. Press 'MATCH' and 'START/STOP' to cook the beans
5. Give the beans a shake at the half way point of cooking
6. Retrieve the beans and serve

Corn-On-Cob

Serves 10

Prep time: 2 minutes | Cook time: 8 minutes

Ingredients:
- 10 corn ears
- 120g butter
- 120g sour cream and chives

Preparation Instructions:
1. Preheat the dual zone to 190°C for 5 minutes
2. Place the 5 corn ears in each draw of the dual zone and layer the butter on top
3. Pair the zone draws to 'ROAST' at 190°C for 9 minutes, then press 'MATCH' and 'START/STOP'
4. At the 4 minute mark of cooking flip the corn ears
5. Once done, remove the corn ears then top with sour cream and chives to serve amongst the family

Green Beans & Lemon Wedges

Serves 4

Prep time: 10 minutes | Cook time: 10 minutes

Ingredients:
- 500g raw green beans
- 1 tbsp olive oil
- ½ tsp sea salt
- ½ tap ground black pepper

Preparation Instructions:
1. Preheat the air fryer at 180°C for 5 minutes
2. Meanwhile, wash the green beans, then slice off their stems
3. Toss the green beans into a large mixing bowl, followed by salt, pepper and olive oil
4. Amalgamate the Ingredients using a wooden spoon
5. The next destination for the green beans is the is the duel zone draws (half in each zone draw)
6. Pair the zone draws to 'ROAST' at 180°C for 8 minutes
7. Press 'MATCH' followed by 'START/STOP' to begin cooking the green beans
8. Meanwhile, cut a lemon into 4 wedges
9. At the 4 minutes, give the zone draws a shake
10. Retrieve the green beans and divide them on to 4 places with a lemon wedge, before serving

Spicy White Kidney Beans

Serves 5

Prep time: 5 minutes | Cook time: 15 minutes

Ingredients:
- 500g white kidney beans
- 1 tbsp olive oil
- 1 tsp honey
- ¼ tsp Worchester sauce
- ¼ tsp cayenne pepper
- ¼ tsp ground cumin
- ¼ tsp paprika
- ½ tsp garam masala
- ¼ tsp garlic powder
- ¼ tsp onion powder
- ¼ tsp dried thyme
- ¼ tsp dried oregano
- ¼ tsp sea salt
- 1/8 tsp black pepper, grounded
- 1/8 tsp ginger grounded
- 10g coriander leaves, diced

Preparation Instructions:
1. Amalgamate all of the Ingredients into a medium sized mixing bowl
2. Make sure you coat the white kidney beans thoroughly by folding them into the spices
3. Place a crisper plate in the zone draws of the ninja foodi, then toss in chickpeas
4. Set the zones by pairing them to 'ROAST' at 200°C for 15 minutes
5. Press 'MATCH' followed by 'STOP/START to air fry the white kidney beans
6. Pull out the draws and shake the white kidney beans at the 7 minute mark
7. Retrieve the spicy white kidney beans, top with coriander leaves then serve

Chapter 3: Meat Recipes

Crispy Chicken Wings

Servings: 2
Prep time: 5 minutes / Cook time: 35 minutes

Ingredients:
- Chicken Wings
- Aluminium-free Baking Powder
- Olive Oil
- Black Pepper
- Sea Salt

Preparation Procedures

1. Take out paper towels and pat dry the chicken wings you will use. Ensure you pat very dry, increasing the chances of the chicken getting more crispy.
2. Add baking powder, sea salt, olive oil and black pepper into a bowl. Put the chicken wings into this mixture and mix thoroughly.
3. When you're done mixing, take out the non-stick plates in your Ninja Dual Zone Air Fryer and arrange the chicken wings on it. Ensure the chicken wings don't touch.
4. If the chicken wings are too much to fit, cook in different batches.
5. Set the Ninja Dual Zone Air Fryer to "Air Fry" and air fry for 15 minutes at 130C. If the chicken wings were frozen, air fry for an additional 10 minutes before flipping.
6. Flip the chicken wings to the other side and increase the temperature of your Ninja Dual Zone Air Fryer to the highest value.
7. Air fry the chicken wings for 18 mins.
8. Take out your crispy chicken wings and enjoy.

Lemon Herb Air Fryer Chicken Breast

Servings: 2
Prep time: 35 minutes / Cook time: 16 minutes

Ingredients
For The Marinade
- Rosemary
- Dried Thyme
- Lemon Juice
- Parsley
- Black Pepper
- Lemon Zest
- Olive Oil
- Rosemary

For The Chicken
- Chicken Breast
- Garlic Poweder
- Thyme
- Salt to taste

Preparation Procedures

1. Use a kitchen towel to lay the chicken breasts dry.
2. Mix the Garlic powder, lemon zest, thyme, black pepper, lemon juice, rosemary, salt, oil and parsley. This will be the marinade.
3. Pour the marinade into the chicken breasts and incorporate thoroughly into it by rubbing it into the chicken.
4. Use some clingfilm to cover the bowl. Place the marinated chicken breasts in the fridge and allow them to sit for about 30 minutes or more.
5. When it's marinated for at least 30 minutes or as long as you'd like, take it out and prepare your air fryer.
6. Turn on your Ninja Dual Zone Air Fryer, select the zone you want to cook it in and set it to "AIR FRY".
7. Arrange the marinated chicken breasts on the non stick plates and place into the air fryer drawers.
8. Set the air fryer's temperature to 180C and air fry the chicken breasts for 8 minutes.
9. Flip over the chicken when the first 8 minutes are done and air fry the other side for 8 minutes.
10. When this is complete, take the chicken out of the air fryer and allow it to sit before it's ready to be served.

Garlic Parmesan Air Fryer Chicken Tenders

Servings: 2
Prep time: 35 minutes / Cook time: 16 minutes

Ingredients
- 680g chicken tenders
- 250g all-purpose flour
- 3 eggs, beaten

- 50g bread crumbs
- 50g grated Parmesan cheese
- 3 cloves garlic, minced
- 1 teaspoon dried parsley
- 1/2 teaspoon salt
- 1/4 teaspoon black pepper
- Cooking spray

Preparation Procedures

1. Preheat the Ninja Dual Zone Air Fryer to 200°C..
2. Combine the bread crumbs, grated Parmesan cheese, minced garlic, dried parsley, salt, and black pepper in a shallow bowl or dish. Mix well.
3. Place the all-purpose flour in a separate shallow bowl or dish.
4. Dip each chicken tender into the flour, shaking off any excess. Then dip it into the beaten eggs, allowing any excess to drip off.
5. Adter the draining, roll the chicken tender in the bread crumb mixture, pressing gently to hold on to the coating. Repeat this process for all the chicken tenders.
6. Spray the Air Fryer non-stick plates with cooking spray to prevent sticking.
7. Place the chicken tenders in a single layer in the Air Fryer drawers, leaving space between them for proper air circulation. You might need to cook the chicken tenders in batches.
8. Insert the drawer into the Ninja Dual Zone Air Fryer and set the timer for 10 minutes.
9. After 10 minutes, remove the non-stick plates from the Air Fryer and flip the chicken tenders to ensure even cooking. Return them to the Air Fryer.
10. Continue cooking for 5-7 minutes, or until the chicken tenders are golden brown and cooked through.
11. Once cooked, remove the chicken tenders from the Air Fryer and let them rest for a few minutes.
12. Serve the Garlic Parmesan Air Fryer Chicken Tenders hot with your favorite dipping sauces, such as marinara sauce, ranch dressing, or honey mustard.

Honey Mustard Glazed Air Fryer Turkey Breast

Servings: 2
Prep time: 10 minutes / Cook time: 50 minutes

Ingredients
- Turkey whole breast
- Butter
- Fresh herbs chopped rosemary, thyme, sage
- Olive oil
- Honey
- Salt
- Black pepper
- Dijon mustard

Preparation Procedures:

1. Preheat your Ninja Dual Zone Air Fryer to 130C.
2. Get hold of a pair of scissors, sharp ones, and slice down mid-turkey to divide the breasts into two.
3. Dab some olive oil all over the turkey breast. Combine salt, chopped herbs, and pepper in a separate bowl. Rub in the herb mixture over the turkey breast.
4. Put each half in the two zones of your Ninja Dual Zone Air Fryer. Set the air Fryer to "Air Fry" and cook the turkey for 20 minutes.
5. Flip the turkey breast to the opposite side and cook the other side for another 15 minutes.
6. While the turkey air fries, mix butter, mustard and honey in a saucepan using medium heat.
7. When the butter melts completely, whisk the mixture to combine properly.
8. Take out the turkey breast and glaze it entirely using the honey mustard mixture. Return this into the air Fryer and cook for 5 minutes until brown.
9. Do this same procedure with the second turkey breast.
10. You can use aluminium foil to cover the turkey before you slice it up and serve.

Crispy Coconut Air Fryer Chicken Strips

Servings: 2
Prep time: 35 minutes / Cook time: 16 minutes

Ingredients
- 680g chicken breast, cut into strips
- 250g all-purpose flour
- 3 eggs, beaten
- 135g unsweetened shredded coconut
- 30g panko breadcrumbs
- 1 teaspoon garlic powder
- 1/2 teaspoon salt

- 1/4 teaspoon black pepper
- Olive oil

Preparations Procedure:

1. Preheat your Ninja Dual Zone Air Fryer to 200°C.
2. Mix the shredded coconut, panko breadcrumbs, garlic powder, salt, and black pepper in a bowl.
3. Prepare the all-purpose flour in a different dish.
4. Take each chicken strip and put into the flour. Shake off any excess, then dip into the beaten eggs. Allow the chicken strips to drip off any extra eggs.
5. Roll the chicken strip in the coconut and breadcrumb mixture. Press the chicken strip gently to ensure the coconut and breadcrumb coating stick well. Do this for all the chicken strips.
6. Brush the Air Fryer non stick plates with olive oil to prevent sticking.
7. Arrange the chicken strips in a single layer in the Air Fryer drawers, leaving space between them for proper air circulation.
8. Set the timer for the Air Fryer for 10 minutes and cook.
9. When it's up to 10 minutes, take out the drawer from the Air Fryer and flip the chicken strips. Return them to the Air Fryer.
10. Continue cooking for an additional 5-7 minutes.
11. Once cooked, allow the chicken strips to rest for a few minutes.
12. Serve the Crispy Coconut Air Fryer Chicken Strips while hot, accompanied by your preferred dipping sauce..

Greek Marinated Air Fryer Lamb Chops

Servings: 2
Prep time: 35 minutes / Cook time: 16 minutes

Ingredients
- 4 lamb chops
- 30 ml olive oil
- 30 ml lemon juice
- 2 cloves garlic, minced
- Dried oregano
- Dried thyme
- Dried rosemary
- Salt
- Black pepper

- Lemon wedges, for serving
- Fresh parsley, chopped (optional, for garnish)

Preparation Procedures

1. Combine the olive oil, lemon juice, minced garlic, dried oregano, dried thyme, rosemary, salt, and black pepper in a bowl. Whisk well to combine and create the marinade.
2. Place the lamb chops in a shallow dish or a resealable plastic bag. Pour the marinade over the lamb chops, ensuring they are evenly coated. Cover the dish or seal the bag and refrigerate for at least 2 hours, or overnight for best results. This allows the flavors to penetrate the meat.
3. Preheat your air fryer to 200°C for about 5 minutes.
4. Remove the lamb chops from the marinade, allowing any excess marinade to drip off. Place the lamb chops in a single layer in the air fryer basket, ensuring they are not overcrowded.
5. Place the non stick plates in the air fryer and cook the lamb chops for 10-12 minutes. Flip the chops halfway through the cooking time.
6. Once cooked, remove the lamb chops from the air fryer and let them rest for a few minutes before serving. This allows the juices to redistribute and ensures that the lamb is tender and juicy.
7. Eat the Greek marinated lamb chops hot, and garnish it with lemon wedges and chopped parsley.

Rosemary Garlic Air Fryer Lamb Steaks

Servings: 2
Prep time: 35 minutes / Cook time: 16 minutes

Ingredients
- 2 lamb steaks (about 200 grams each)
- 30 ml olive oil
- 2 cloves of garlic, minced
- 15 ml lemon juice
- 5 grams fresh rosemary leaves, chopped
- 5 grams salt
- 2 grams black pepper
- Cooking spray or oil for greasing the air fryer basket

Preparation Instructions:

1. Combine the olive oil, minced garlic, lemon juice, chopped rosemary leaves, salt, and black pepper in a small bowl. Mix well to create a

marinade for the lamb steaks.

2. Place the lamb steaks in a shallow dish and pour the marinade over them, ensuring both sides are coated. Allow the lamb to marinate at room temperature for at least 30 minutes, or refrigerate for a couple of hours for a stronger flavor.

3. Preheat your air fryer to 200°C (400°F) for about 5 minutes.

4. Lightly grease the air fryer basket with cooking spray or oil to prevent the lamb steaks from sticking.

5. Place the marinated lamb steaks in the air fryer basket in a single layer.

6. Cook the lamb steaks in the air fryer for 8-10 minutes for medium-rare, or adjust the cooking time according to your preferred level of doneness. Flip the steaks halfway through the cooking time to ensure even browning.

7. Once cooked, remove the lamb steaks from the air fryer and let them rest for a few minutes before serving.

8. Slice the lamb steaks against the grain and serve them as a main course.

Mint and Yogurt Marinated Air Fryer Lamb Kebabs

Servings: 2
Prep time: 5 minutes / Cook time: 10 minutes

Ingredients

- 300 grams lamb, cut into 1-inch cubes
- 240ml plain yogurt
- 2 tablespoons olive oil
- 3 cloves garlic, minced
- Fresh mint, finely chopped
- Fresh cilantro, finely chopped
- Fresh lemon juice
- Ground cumin
- Ground coriander
- Paprika
- Salt
- Black pepper

Preparation Procedures:

1. Combine the yogurt, olive oil, minced garlic, fresh mint, fresh cilantro, lemon juice, ground cumin, coriander, paprika, salt, and black pepper in a bowl. Mix well to create the marinade.

2. Place the lamb cubes in a shallow dish or a resealable plastic bag. Pour the marinade over the lamb, ensuring all the pieces are evenly coated.

3. Cover the dish or seal the bag and refrigerate for at least 2 hours, or overnight for best results. This allows the flavors to infuse into the meat.

4. Preheat your air fryer to 200°C for about 5 minutes.

5. Thread the marinated lamb cubes onto skewers, leaving a small gap between each piece for even cooking. If using bamboo skewers, soak them in water for 30 minutes beforehand to prevent burning.

6. Place the skewers in a single layer in the air fryer basket, ensuring they are not overcrowded.

7. Place the basket in the air fryer and cook the lamb kebabs at 200°C for 8-10 minutes. Flip the kebabs halfway through the cooking time to ensure even browning.

8. Once cooked, remove the lamb kebabs from the air fryer and let them rest.

9. Serve the Mint and Yogurt Marinated Air Fryer Lamb Kebabs hot, garnished with a sprinkle of fresh mint or cilantro.

Spicy Harissa Air Fryer Lamb Burgers

Servings: 2
Prep time: 5 minutes / Cook time: 12 minutes

Ingredients:
For the lamb burgers:
- 300 grams ground lamb
- 30 grams harissa paste
- ½ cloves garlic, minced
- Ground cumin
- Ground coriander
- Salt
- Black pepper
- Paprika
- 2 hamburger buns

For the toppings:
- Lettuce leaves
- Sliced tomatoes
- Sliced red onions
- Pickles

For the harissa aioli:
- 120 ml mayonnaise
- 15 ml harissa paste

- 1 clove garlic, minced
- 15 ml lemon juice
- Salt and pepper to taste

Preparation Procedures:

1. Preheat your Air Fryer to 200°C.
2. Combine ground lamb, harissa paste, minced garlic, cumin, coriander, salt, black pepper, and paprika in a large mixing bowl. Mix well until all the Ingredients are evenly incorporated.
3. Divide the lamb mixture into four equal portions. Shape each portion into a patty, about ¾ inch thick. Ensure the patties are slightly larger than the hamburger buns since they will shrink during cooking.
4. Lightly spray the air fryer basket with cooking oil spray to prevent sticking. Place the lamb patties in the basket, leaving some space between each patty.
5. Insert the drawer into the Air Fryer, and cook for 8-10 minutes, flipping the patties halfway through the cooking time.
6. While the lamb patties are cooking, prepare the harissa aioli. In a small bowl, combine mayonnaise, harissa paste, minced garlic, lemon juice, salt, and pepper. Stir well to combine. Adjust the seasonings according to your taste.
7. Once the lamb patties are cooked to your desired level, remove them from the air fryer and let them rest for a few minutes.
8. While the patties are resting, lightly toast the hamburger buns in the air fryer for about 1-2 minutes.
9. To assemble the burgers, spread a generous amount of harissa aioli on the bottom half of each toasted bun. Place a lamb patty on top of the aioli, and then add lettuce, sliced tomatoes, sliced red onions, and pickles. You can add additional condiments or toppings according to your preference.
10. Finally, place the top half of the bun on the assembled burger, and secure it with a toothpick if needed.
11. Serve the Spicy Harissa Air Fryer Lamb Burgers immediately to enjoy this wonderful recipe.

Moroccan Spiced Air Fryer Lamb Meatballs

Servings: 2
Prep time: 5 minutes / Cook time: 15 minutes

Ingredients

- 500 grams ground lamb
- 30 grams bread crumbs
- 1 small onion, finely chopped
- 2 cloves of garlic, minced
- 15 grams fresh cilantro, chopped
- 15 grams fresh parsley, chopped
- 10 grams ground cumin
- 5 grams ground coriander
- 5 grams paprika
- 5 grams ground cinnamon
- 5 grams salt
- 2 grams ground black pepper
- 30 ml olive oil
- Cooking spray or oil for greasing the air fryer basket.

Preparation Instructions:

1. In a large mixing bowl, combine the ground lamb, bread crumbs, chopped onion, minced garlic, chopped cilantro, chopped parsley, ground cumin, ground coriander, paprika, ground cinnamon, salt, and black pepper. Mix well until all the Ingredients are evenly combined.
2. Shape the mixture into small meatballs, about 1 inch in diameter. You can use your hands or a small cookie scoop to portion the lamb mixture.
3. Preheat your air fryer to 180°C for about 5 minutes.
4. Lightly grease the air fryer basket with cooking spray or oil to prevent the meatballs from sticking.
5. Place the meatballs in a single layer in the air fryer basket, leaving space between them for proper airflow.
6. Cook the meatballs in the air fryer for 12-15 minutes, shaking the basket or flipping the meatballs halfway through the cooking time to ensure even browning.
7. Once cooked, remove the meatballs from the air fryer and let them rest for a few minutes before serving.

Classic Air Fryer Beef Burgers

Servings: 2
Prep time: 10 minutes / Cook time: 12 minutes

Ingredients

- 500 grams ground beef

- 1 small onion, finely chopped
- 1 clove of garlic, minced
- 15 ml Worcestershire sauce
- 15 ml ketchup
- 5 ml Dijon mustard
- 5 ml soy sauce
- 5 grams dried oregano
- 5 grams dried basil
- 5 grams salt
- 2 grams black pepper
- Cooking spray or oil for greasing the air fryer basket
- Burger buns and toppings (lettuce, tomato, cheese, etc.)

Preparation Instructions:

1. In a large mixing bowl, combine the ground beef, chopped onion, minced garlic, Worcestershire sauce, ketchup, Dijon mustard, soy sauce, dried oregano, dried basil, salt, and black pepper. Mix well until all the Ingredients are evenly combined.
2. Divide the mixture into equal portions and shape them into burger patties. Make sure the patties are slightly larger than your burger buns, as they will shrink slightly during cooking.
3. Preheat your air fryer to 200°C for about 5 minutes.
4. Lightly grease the air fryer non stick plates with cooking spray or oil to prevent the burgers from sticking.
5. Place the burger patties in a single layer in the air fryer basket, ensuring they are not touching each other.
6. Cook the burgers in the air fryer for 10-12 minutes, flipping them halfway through the cooking time to ensure even browning. Adjust the cooking time based on your preferred level of doneness.
7. When cooked, remove the burgers from the air fryer and rest for a few minutes.
8. Assemble your burgers by placing the cooked patties on the burger buns and adding your desired toppings such as lettuce, tomato, cheese, and condiments.
9. Serve the Classic Air Fryer Beef Burgers with fries or a fresh salad.

Asian Style Air Fryer Beef Stir-Fry

Servings: 2
Prep time: 28 minutes / Cook time: 6 minutes

Ingredients:

- 350 g beef steak (such as sirloin or flank), thinly sliced
- 2 tablespoons soy sauce
- 1 tablespoon oyster sauce
- 1 tablespoon hoisin sauce
- 1 tablespoon rice vinegar
- 2 teaspoons sesame oil
- 2 teaspoons cornstarch
- 1 teaspoon grated ginger
- 2 cloves garlic, minced
- 1 Yellow, Red and Green bell pepper each, thinly sliced
- 1 medium onion, thinly sliced
- 100g snap peas
- 1 tablespoon vegetable oil
- Optional garnish: sliced green onions and sesame seeds

Preparation Procedures

1. Mix the soy sauce, oyster sauce, hoisin sauce, rice vinegar, sesame oil, cornstarch, grated ginger, and minced garlic in a bowl. Stir well to create a marinade for the beef.
2. Add the thinly sliced beef to the marinade and toss until all the slices are well coated. Let the beef marinate for at least 20 minutes, soaking up the flavors.
3. Preheat your air fryer to 200°C for a few minutes.
4. While the air fryer heats up, heat the vegetable oil in a large skillet or wok over medium-high heat. Add the bell peppers, onion, and snap peas, and stir-fry for 3-4 minutes until they soften. Remove the vegetables from the skillet and set them aside.
5. Add the marinated beef slices in the same skillet and cook for 3-4 minutes. Make sure to discard any excess marinade.
6. Transfer the cooked beef to the preheated air fryer basket, spreading it in a single layer. Cook for 5-6 minutes, shaking the basket or flipping the beef halfway through, until the beef is crispy and browned.
7. Return the cooked vegetables to the skillet with the beef and toss them together for a minute to combine and reheat.
8. Once the beef and vegetables are thoroughly combined, remove from heat and serve the Asian

style stir-fry immediately.

9. If desired, you can garnish your stir fry with sliced green onions and sesame seeds.

Garlic Butter Air Fryer Steak Bites

Ingredients:
- 500 g beef sirloin or ribeye steak, cut into bite-sized pieces
- 30 g unsalted butter, melted
- 3 cloves of garlic, minced
- 15 ml olive oil
- 5 ml Worcestershire sauce
- 5 ml soy sauce
- 1/2 teaspoon salt
- 1/4 teaspoon black pepper
- Cooking spray or oil for greasing the air fryer basket
- Fresh parsley, chopped (for garnish, optional)

Preparation Procedures

1. Preheat your air fryer to 200°C (400°F) for about 5 minutes.
2. Combine the melted butter, minced garlic, olive oil, Worcestershire sauce, soy sauce, salt, and black pepper in a mixing bowl. Mix well to create the garlic butter marinade.
3. Add the bite-sized steak pieces to the garlic butter marinade and toss until all the steak pieces are evenly coated. Allow the steak to marinate at room temperature for 15-20 minutes, or refrigerate for a couple of hours for a stronger flavor.
4. Lightly grease the air fryer basket with cooking spray or oil to prevent the steak bites from sticking.
5. Place the marinated steak bites in a single layer in the air fryer basket, making sure not to overcrowd them. You may need to cook them in batches depending on the size of your air fryer.
6. Cook the steak bites in the air fryer for 8-10 minutes, flipping them halfway through the cooking time to ensure even browning. Adjust the cooking time based on your desired level of doneness.
7. Once cooked, remove the steak bites from the air fryer and let them rest for a few minutes.
8. Serve the Garlic Butter Air Fryer Steak Bites and garnish them with fresh chopped parsley, if you prefer.

Korean BBQ Air Fryer Beef Skewers

Ingredients:
- 500 g beef sirloin, thinly sliced
- 60 ml soy sauce
- 30 ml mirin
- 30 ml sesame oil
- 30 ml honey
- 2 cloves of garlic, minced
- 15 ml rice vinegar
- 15 ml gochujang (Korean red pepper paste)
- 1 tablespoon sesame seeds
- 1/2 teaspoon black pepper
- 1/4 teaspoon salt
- Bamboo skewers, soaked in water for 30 minutes
- Cooking spray or oil for greasing the air fryer basket
- Chopped green onions (for garnish, optional)

Preparation Instruction

1. Combine the soy sauce, mirin, sesame oil, honey, minced garlic, rice vinegar, gochujang, sesame seeds, black pepper, and salt in a mixing bowl. Mix well to create the Korean BBQ marinade.
2. Add the thinly sliced beef to the marinade, ensuring each slice is evenly coated. Let the beef marinate in the refrigerator for at least 1 hour or overnight for more flavor.
3. Preheat your air fryer to 200°C for about 5 minutes.
4. Thread the marinated beef slices onto the soaked bamboo skewers, ensuring they are evenly distributed.
5. Lightly grease the air fryer basket with cooking spray or oil to prevent the skewers from sticking.
6. Place the beef skewers in a single layer in the air fryer basket, ensuring they are not touching each other.
7. Cook the beef skewers in the air fryer for 6-8 minutes, flipping them halfway through the cooking time to ensure even browning. Adjust the cooking time based on your preferred level of doneness.
8. Once cooked, remove the beef skewers from the air fryer and let them rest for a few minutes.

Italian Seasoned Air Fryer Meatballs

Servings: 2
Prep time: 5 minutes / Cook time: 15 minutes

Ingredients:

- 500 g ground beef
- 50 g bread crumbs
- 50 g grated Parmesan cheese
- 1 small onion, finely chopped
- 2 cloves of garlic, minced
- 1 egg
- 30 ml milk
- 1 tablespoon fresh parsley, chopped
- 1 teaspoon dried oregano
- 1 teaspoon dried basil
- 1/2 teaspoon salt
- 1/4 teaspoon black pepper
- Cooking spray or oil for greasing the air fryer basket

Preparation Procedures

1. In a large mixing bowl, combine the ground beef, bread crumbs, grated Parmesan cheese, chopped onion, minced garlic, egg, milk, chopped parsley, dried oregano, dried basil, salt, and black pepper. Mix well until all the Ingredients are evenly combined.
2. Shape the mixture into small meatballs, about 1 inch in diameter. You can use your hands or a small cookie scoop to portion the meat mixture.
3. Preheat your air fryer to 180°C for about 5 minutes.
4. Lightly grease the air fryer drawers and non stick plates with cooking spray or oil to prevent the meatballs from sticking.
5. Place the meatballs in a single layer in the air fryer basket, leaving space between them for proper airflow.
6. Cook the meatballs in the air fryer for 12-15 minutes, shaking the basket or flipping the meatballs halfway through the cooking time to ensure even browning.
7. Once cooked, remove the meatballs from the air fryer and let them rest for a few minutes before serving.
8. Serve the Italian seasoned air fryer meatballs as an appetizer, with pasta, or as a sandwich filling.

Crispy Air Fryer Pork Chops

Servings: 2
Prep time: 5 minutes / Cook time: 15 minutes

Ingredients:

- 2 pork chops (about 200 g each)

- 30 g breadcrumbs
- 15 g grated Parmesan cheese
- 5 g paprika
- 5 g garlic powder
- 5 g dried thyme
- 5 g salt
- 2 g black pepper
- Cooking spray or oil for greasing the air fryer basket

Preparation Instructions:

1. Combine the bread crumbs, grated Parmesan cheese, paprika, garlic powder, dried thyme, salt, and black pepper in a shallow dish. Mix well to create the coating mixture for the pork chops.
2. Pat dry the pork chops with a paper towel to remove excess moisture.
3. Lightly grease the air fryer basket with cooking spray or oil to prevent the pork chops from sticking.
4. Dredge each pork chop in the coating mixture, pressing it gently to adhere.
5. Place the coated pork chops in the air fryer basket in a single layer.
6. Cook the pork chops in the air fryer at 200°C for 12-15 minutes, flipping them halfway through the cooking time to ensure even browning. Adjust the cooking time based on the thickness of the pork chops.
7. Once cooked, remove the pork chops from the air fryer and let them rest for a few minutes before serving.
8. Serve the Crispy Air Fryer Pork Chops with your favorite side dishes such as mashed potatoes, roasted vegetables, or a fresh salad.

Honey Garlic Air Fryer Pork Tenderloin

Servings: 2
Prep time: 5 minutes / Cook time: 25 minutes

Ingredients:

- 500 g pork tenderloin
- 60 ml honey
- 30 ml soy sauce
- 15 ml rice vinegar
- 15 ml olive oil
- 3 cloves of garlic, minced

- 5 g ginger, grated
- 2 g black pepper
- Cooking spray or oil for greasing the air fryer basket

Preparation Instructions:

1. Combine the honey, soy sauce, rice vinegar, olive oil, minced garlic, grated ginger, and black pepper in a mixing bowl. Mix well to create the marinade for the pork tenderloin.
2. Place the pork tenderloin in a shallow dish and pour the marinade over it, ensuring all sides are coated. Let the pork marinate for at least 30 minutes, or refrigerate it for a few hours to enhance the flavor.
3. Preheat your air fryer to 200°C for about 5 minutes.
4. Lightly grease the air fryer basket with cooking spray or oil to prevent the pork tenderloin from sticking.
5. Place the marinated pork tenderloin in the air fryer basket.
6. Cook the pork tenderloin in the air fryer for 20-25 minutes, Flip the tenderloin halfway through the cooking time for even browning.
7. Once cooked, remove the pork tenderloin from the air fryer and let it rest for a few minutes before slicing.
8. Slice the Honey Garlic Air Fryer Pork Tenderloin and serve it as a main course. Drizzle any remaining marinade over the sliced pork for added flavor

BBQ Rubbed Air Fryer Pork Ribs

Servings: 2
Prep time: 5 minutes / Cook time: 35 minutes

Ingredients:

- 800 g pork ribs
- 60 g brown sugar
- 15 g smoked paprika
- 15 g garlic powder
- 10 g onion powder
- 5 g salt
- 5 g black pepper
- 30 ml olive oil
- BBQ sauce for serving

Preparation Instructions:

1. Preheat your Ninja Dual Zone air fryer to 180°C.
2. Combine the brown sugar, smoked paprika, garlic

powder, onion powder, salt, and black pepper in a bowl to make the BBQ rub.
3. Rub the olive oil all over the pork ribs to help the rub stick.
4. Generously coat the pork ribs with the BBQ rub, ensuring that both sides are well-covered.
5. Place the ribs in the air fryer basket, ensuring they are not overcrowded.
6. Air fry the ribs for 30-35 minutes, flipping them halfway through cooking.
7. Once the ribs are cooked and tender, remove them from the air fryer.
8. Let the ribs rest for a few minutes, then serve hot with additional BBQ sauce on the side.

Sweet and Sour Air Fryer Pork Belly

Servings: 2
Prep time: 5 minutes / Cook time: 20 minutes

Ingredients:

- 500 g pork belly, sliced into bite-sized pieces
- 60 ml soy sauce
- 60 ml rice vinegar
- 60 ml pineapple juice
- 60 g brown sugar
- 30 ml ketchup
- 15 ml honey
- 10 g cornstarch
- 30 ml water
- Vegetable oil for brushing

Preparation Procedures

1. Preheat your Ninja Dual Zone air fryer to 200°C.
2. In a bowl, combine the soy sauce, rice vinegar, pineapple juice, brown sugar, ketchup, and honey to make the sweet and sour sauce and set it aside.
3. Brush the pork belly slices with a little vegetable oil.
4. Place the pork belly slices in the air fryer basket in a single layer, without overcrowding.
5. Air fry the pork belly for 10 minutes, then flip the slices and air fry for 10 minutes until they are crispy and golden brown.
6. While the pork belly is cooking, prepare the sweet and sour sauce. In a small saucepan, mix the cornstarch with water until smooth.
7. Add the sweet and sour sauce mixture to the

saucepan and cook over medium heat until it thickens, stirring constantly.

8. Once the pork belly is cooked, remove it from the air fryer and place it in a bowl.

9. Pour the sweet and sour sauce over the pork belly and toss gently to coat.

10. Serve the sweet and sour pork belly hot, garnished with chopped green onions or sesame seeds if desired

Teriyaki Glazed Air Fryer Pork Skewers

Servings: 2

Prep time: 5 minutes / Cook time: 12 minutes

Ingredients:
- 600 g pork loin, cut into 2 cm cubes
- 60 ml soy sauce
- 30 ml mirin
- 30 ml sake (Japanese rice wine)
- 30 ml honey
- 15 ml sesame oil
- 5 g ginger, grated
- 2 cloves garlic, minced
- 10 ml vegetable oil for brushing
- Sesame seeds and chopped green onions for garnish

Preparation Instructions:

1. Combine the soy sauce, mirin, sake, honey, sesame oil, grated ginger, and minced garlic in a bowl to make the teriyaki marinade.

2. Add the pork loin cubes to the marinade, ensuring they are well coated. Let the pork marinate in the refrigerator for at least 30 minutes or overnight for maximum flavor.

3. Preheat the air fryer to 200°C

4. Thread the marinated pork cubes onto skewers, about 4-5 pieces per skewer. Discard any excess marinade.

5. Lightly brush the air fryer basket with vegetable oil to prevent sticking.

6. Place the pork skewers in the air fryer basket in a single layer, without overcrowding. Cook in batches if necessary.

7. Air fry the pork skewers for 10-12 minutes, turning them halfway through the cooking time to ensure even browning.

8. While the pork skewers are cooking, pour the

remaining marinade into a small saucepan and simmer over medium heat until it thickens into a glaze.

9. Once the pork skewers are cooked and nicely browned, remove them from the air fryer.

10. Brush the cooked pork skewers with the teriyaki glaze, or drizzle the glaze over the skewers.

11. Garnish with sesame seeds and chopped green onions.

12. Serve your teriyaki glazed pork skewers hot as an appetizer or a main dish with steamed rice and vegetables.

British Haslet Duo (Pork and Beef)

Serves 12

Prep time: 20 minutes | Cook time: 105 minutes

Ingredients:

For Pork Haslet
- 1000g finely chopped pork belly
- 250g finely chopped onion
- 2 large beaten egg
- 50g day old dry bread crumbs
- 2 tbsp chopped sage
- 2 tsp sea salt
- 2 tsp ground black pepper
- 3 tbsp olive oil

For Beef Haslet
- 500g beef mince (80% beef)
- 125g finely chopped onion
- 1 large beaten egg
- 25g bread crumbs
- 1 tbsp chopped thyme
- 1 tsp sea salt
- 1 tsp ground black pepper
- 2 mushrooms sliced into wedges
- 1 ½ tbsp flaxseed oil

Preparation Instructions:

1. Place the crisper plates in the ninja foodi and start preheating the unit at 200°C for 4-5 minutes

2. Toss the pork meat into a large bowl, add the onions, bread crumbs, egg, thyme, salt and pepper. Hand mix and amalgamate the Ingredients

3. Dollop this pork mixture into a large loaf pan (if suitable for your air fryer), loaf pans brush the pork over with oil

4. Place the haslet it into zone 1 and cover it with foil

5. Now toss the minced beef into a large bowl, add the onions, bread crumbs, egg, thyme, salt and pepper. Hand mix and amalgamate the Ingredients

6. Dollop this meat mixture into the ninja foodi and pierce mushrooms into the slab of meat and brush them over it with oil

7. Select zone 1 and pair it with 'ROAST' at 200°C for 60 minutes 60 minutes

8. Select zone 2 and pair it with 'ROAST' at 200°C for 25 minutes

9. Press 'SYNC' and 'START/STOP' to begin roasting the zone 1 haslet

10. After the zone 1 pork content has cooked for 60 minutes, remove the foil and cook for another 45 minutes

11. Retrieve the haslets and set them aside to cool

12. Slice each pork haslet into 8 portions and the beef into 4, then serve

Chicken Lasagne

Serves 6

Prep time: 75 minutes | Cook time: 75 minutes

Ingredients:

- 500g chicken breast mince
- 2 crushed garlic cloves
- tsp dried oregano or dried mixed herbs
- 500g sliced mushrooms
- 400ml vegetable broth
- 50g tomato ketchup
- 1 large egg
- 300ml double cream
- 200g grated British mature cheddar
- 9 sheets of fresh lasagne
- ¾ nutmeg

Preparation Instructions:

1. Preheat the ninja for 4-5 minutes at 180°C

2. Place 125g of chicken mince in each ninja foodi zone. Pair the ninja with 'AIR FRY' at 180°C for 6 minutes. Press 'MATCH' followed by 'STOP/START'

3. Pull our the zone draws every 2 minutes and shake the food content. After 6 minutes, retrieve the cooked mince and place it in a bowl

4. Repeat this process with the other 250g of mince in both ninja zones using the same function and time , but add garlic and oregano

5. Toss in the browned portion of mince with mushrooms, veg broth, ketchup and the remainder seasoning, divided between both zone draws

6. Pair the 'AIR FRY' function for the third time at 180°C for 30 minutes, making sure you shake the food content in the zone draws every 10 minutes

7. In the mean time, use a stand mixer on the slow setting, combine double cream and 100g of cheese and an egg, making a cheese sauce. Layer a dish with lasagne and add boiling to pre-cook for 5 minutes

8. Retrieve the chicken mince mix, then spread 2 heaped wooden spoons on 2 ninja baking trays suitable for the ninja draws

9. Using kitchen tongs, layer 3 sheets of lasagne (cut if needed) onto this meat mix. Drizzle 4 tbsp of the cheese on top of the lasagne sheets, then dollop and spread half of the remaining chicken mix

10. Apply another layer of lasagne (3 sheets). Once again, dollop and spread the remaining meat mix, followed by the last 3 sheets of lasagne

11. Pour the rest of the cheese sauce evenly over the last layer of lasagne. To finalise, sprinkle the remaining 100g of cheddar and nutmeg over the top of the bake.

12. Place 1 baking dishes in each zone draw and pair them with 'BAKE' at 180°C for 25 minutes

13. Retrieve the dishes and cut 3 squares out of each to serve

Roast Turkey On Creamy Mash

Serves 4

Prep time: 5 minutes | Cook time: 25 minutess

Ingredients:

For turkey

- 2 large skinless turkey breasts
- 1 thyme sprig
- 1 star anise
- 30g butter

For Mash

- 5 large white potatoes
- 100ml double cream
- 50ml milk
- 1/8 tsp Himalayan salt
- 1/8 tsp ground pepper Preparation Instructions

Preparation Instructions:

1. Preheat the air fryer at 180°C for 5-6 minutes
2. Sprinkle salt and pepper on top of the turkey breasts, then place them in zone 1 of the ninja foodi
3. Create 3 small incisions on the centre of each potato with a knife. This prevents the potatoes from bursting whilst cooking
4. Toss the potatoes in the zone 2 draw of the ninja foodi
5. Select zone 1 and pair it with 'ROAST' at 180°C for 20 minutes, then pair zone 2 with 'BAKE' at 160°C for 25 minutes
6. Press 'SYNC' followed by 'STOP/START' to get cooking
7. Flip the Turkey breasts and dollop butter, thyme, and star anise oat the half way point of cooking
8. Retrieve the food content, split the potatoes in half using a knife and extract the potato mass using a spoon, then toss the potatoes into a mixing bowl
9. Mash the potato and add seasoning, double cream and milk, then stir thoroughly
10. Equally divide the creamy mash on 4 plates and top with half a turkey breast in half
11. Top the turkey with any left over juices in the zone 1 draw, then serve

English Sheppard's Pie

Serves 7

Prep time: 20 minutes | Cook time: 50 minutes

Ingredients:

- 500g British mince lamb
- 240g British mature cheddar
- 30g parmesan cheese
- 900g hash brown
- 120ml lamb broth
- 30g Butter
- 25g cooking flour
- 500g chopped mushrooms
- 15g chopped rosemary
- 30g tomato puree
- ¼ tbsp Himalayan salt
- ½ tbsp ground pepper
- 2 minced garlic cloves
- 100g diced onion
- 100g diced fennel
- 60g diced carrot
- 1 tbsp Worcestershire sauce
- 1 tbsp British mustard
- 2 tbsp fine chopped parsley

Preparation Instructions:

1. First of all, butter a large frying pan and place it on the stove at a 'high heat'
2. Add and stir the mushrooms, followed by 1/8 tbsp of salt and ¼ tbsp of the ground pepper
3. After the 5 minute mark, the mushrooms should begin to appear brown in colour, where you will then need to add and stir the onions, fennel, carrot, and rosemary for 5 minutes
4. Add the remainder of salt and pepper
5. At this point, we need to add and stir the beef mince and cook it until it becomes brown and crumbly in texture (5 minutes)
6. Dollop the tomato purée in and stir for 50-60 seconds
7. Put these Ingredients into the zone draws, followed by lamb broth, mustard and Worchester sauce
8. Stir these Ingredients thoroughly and then pair the zone draws to 'ROAST' at 200°C for 35 minutes
9. Press 'MATCH' followed by 'START/STOP' to begin
10. Meanwhile, using a stand mixer, whisk the flour with 30-50ml of water. Immediately add this mixture to the zone draws and stir
11. Distribute the hash brown and cheddar on the top of the meat-based mixture
12. To finalise the Sheppard's pie, sprinkle with parmesan cheese
13. Once complete, cut each Sheppard's pie into 10 small square to serve

Smoked Pork Ribs

Serves 7

Prep time: 5 minutes | Cook time: 20 minutes

Ingredients:

- 20 pork ribs (2 racks)
- 600g BBQ sauce
- 2 tsp liquid smoke
- 2 tsp sea salt
- 1 tsp black pepper, grounded

Preparation Instructions:

1. Place the pork ribs in a large mixing bowl and dash in the salt, pepper and liquid smoke, then leave the ribs for 5 minutes
2. Follow this by drenching the pork ribs in ¾ of the BBQ sauce and then rub it in
3. Place the 10 ribs in each draws on the dual zone
4. Pair the dual zone to 'ROAST' at 200°C for 20 minutes, then press 'MATCH' and 'STOP/START' to smoke the pork ribs
5. At the 6 minute mark of cooking flip the pork ribs and baste the remainder of the BBQ sauce
6. Once complete, retrieve the smoked pork ribs to serve

British 'Bangers' & Mash Topped With Gravy

Serves 7

Prep time: 30 minutes | Cook time: 55 minutes

Ingredients:

For Sausages
- 10 sausages (meat of choice)
- 20g butter
- 200g finely sliced onion
- 1 thyme sprig
- 1 bay leaf
- 1 tbsp Worchester sauce
- 1 tsp soy sauce
- 400ml beef stock
- 50g finely diced coriander

For Mash
- 10 large white potatoes
- 200ml double cream
- 50ml milk
- 1/8 tsp Himalayan salt
- 1/8 tsp ground pepper

To serve
- 200ml left over gravy, reheated

Preparation Instructions:

1. Preheat the duel zone to 180°C for 4 minutes
2. Create 3 small incisions on the centre of each potato with a knife. This prevents the potatoes from bursting while air frying
3. Toss the potatoes in the zone 1 draw of the air fryer, then place the sausages in the zone 2 draw

4. Pair the zone 1 draw to 'BAKE' at 160°C for 45 minutes and zone 2 to 'AIR FRY' at 180°C for 10 minutes
5. Once done, retrieve the food content, split the potatoes in half using a knife and extract the potato with a tbsp
6. Toss the potato mass into a large mixing bowl and dash in salt and pepper
7. In order to make a creamy mash, add the double cream and milk, then stir thoroughly
8. Set the mash aside in a large dish and cover with foil
9. Toss in onions, butter, sprig, bay leaf, and sausages for the second time in the zone draws
10. Pour in Worchester sauce, soy, and beef stock
11. Pair the zone draws to 'AIR FRY' at 180°C for 10 minutes
12. Remove the Ingredients, dollop and spread them on top of the mash, followed by gravy
13. Serve the traditional 'bangers' and mash on the family dinner table

Traditional Steak and Kidney Pie

Serves 8-10

Prep time: 5 minutes | Cook time: 15 minutes
A close variation to the traditional steak and kidney beans pie, but we have opted tasty prawn cocktail filling.

Ingredients:
- 1 kg steak and kidney filler
- 4 sheet puff pastry
- 1cal olive oil fry spray
- 2 eggs, beaten

Preparation Instructions:

1. Preheat the dual zone to 180° for 6 minutes
2. Meanwhile, cut out 4x6" baking tin shaped pastry's
3. Spray 2 x 6" baking tins thoroughly using the fry spray
4. Fill the ramekins with a layer of pastry then tip with the filling and cover with another layer of pastry
5. Make a small incisions at the centre of the pastries
6. Brush over the top of the pastries with the beaten egg
7. Place a pie in each draw of the dual zone and pair them to 'BAKE' at 180°C for 12-15 minutes
8. Once done, retrieve the steak and cut each pie

into 4-5 slices to serve

Pork Belly & Apple Purée

Serves 6
Prep time: 10 minutes | Cook time: 5-7 minutes

Ingredients:
For Pork
1.5kg Pork Belly
- 2 tbsp olive oil
- 1 tbsp fresh chopped rosemary
- 4 garlic cloves, grated
- ½ tsp sea salt
- ¼ tsp black pepper, grounded

For Apple purée
- 6 cooking bramley apples
- ½ tsp lemon juice
- 1/8 tsp cinnamon
- ½ tsp brown sugar
- 70g butter

Preparation Instructions:
1. Using a large bowl, add the olive oil, garlic and rosemary, then stir into a marinade, then dunk in the pork belly and rub it in thoroughly
2. Cover the bowl with clingfilm and refrigerate the lamb chops 1-2hrs, allowing the flavours to infuse with the pork
3. Place a cake pan in zone 2 draw and preheat it to 200°C for 3-4 minutes
4. Peel and dice the apples, ensuring that you remove the core
5. Toss the apple pieces into the cake pan and pour over hot butter. Stir to combine these Ingredients, then layer the pan with foil and close the zone draw
6. Place the pork belly in the zone 1 draw
7. Pair zone 1 to 'ROAST' at 160°C for 30 minutes and pair zone 2 to 'BAKE' at 180°C for 25 minutes
8. Press 'SYNC' followed by 'START/STOP' to start cooking the pork and apples
9. Receive the food content cooked
10. Place the cooked apples in a large mixing bowl and stir with a wooden spoon to form a thick purée
11. Set the apple sauce aside to cool, sprinkle the sea salt and ground pepper around the pork belly

12. Divide the pork belly between 6 and plate them up with a dollop of apple purée

Greek Lamb Chops & Roasted Baby Carrots

Serves 4
Prep time: 20 minutes | Cook time: 15 minutes

Ingredients:
For lamb
- 8 Lamb chops
- 1 tbsp fresh chopped rosemary
- 1 tbsp rapeseed oil
- 4 grated garlic cloves
- 1 tsp Greek seasoning

For Baby Carrots
- 500g Baby Carrots
- ¼ tsp sea salt
- ¼ tsp garlic powder
- ¼ tsp black pepper, grounded
- 1 tbsp rapeseed oil

Preparation Instructions:
1. Using a large bowl, add oil, garlic and rosemary to stir into a marinade
2. Cover the lamb chops with this marinade, then combine the 'for carrot' Ingredients in a separate bowl
3. Cover both bowls with Clingfilm and refrigerate for 3hrs, allowing the flavours to infuse with the food products
4. Preheat the dual zone at 200°C for 5 minutes
5. Sprinkle the Greek seasoning over the lamb chops
6. Lay the lamb chops in zone 1 and carrots in zone 2 of the dual zone
7. Select zone 1 and pair it with 'ROAST' at 200°C for 10 minutes and zone 2 with 'ROAST' at 210°C for 10 minutes
8. Press 'SYNC' and 'START/STOP' to roast the chops and carrots
9. At the 5 minute mark of roasting, flip the lamb chops and shake the carrots
10. After complete, retrieve the chops and carrots, then divide them on 4 plates to serve

Chapter 4: Fish and Seafood Recipes

Crispy Air-Fried Fish Fillets

Servings: 2
Prep time: 5 mins / Cook time: 12 minutes

Ingredients:
- 400 g fish fillets (such as cod, haddock, or tilapia)
- 60 g all-purpose flour
- Paprika
- Garlic powder
- Onion powder
- Dried thyme
- Salt
- Black pepper
- 1 large egg
- 30 ml milk

Preparation Instructions:
1. Preheat the duel zone to 200°C for about 5 minutes.
2. Pat dry the fish fillets using paper towels to remove any excess moisture. This will ensure the crispiness of the fish.
3. Combine the flour, paprika, garlic powder, onion powder, dried thyme, salt, and black pepper in a shallow bowl.
4. Whisk the egg and milk together until well combined in a different bowl.
5. Dip each fish fillet into the egg mixture, allowing the excess mixture drip off, then coat it evenly with the flour mixture. Brush off the excess flour off the fish.
6. Lightly coat the air fryer drawer and non stick plates with cooking spray to prevent sticking.
7. Place the coated fish fillets in a single layer in the air fryer basket, ensuring they do not overlap.
8. Spray the top of the fillets with cooking spray to help achieve a crispy texture.
9. Air fry the fish fillets at 200°C for 10-12 minutes, flipping them halfway through the cooking time, until they are golden brown and crispy.
10. When they're ready, transfer the crispy air-fried fish fillets to a serving plate and serve them hot.

Cajun Blackened Salmon

Servings: 2
Prep time: 5 mins / Cook time: 8 minutes

Ingredients:
- 300 grams salmon fillets
- Paprika
- Dried thyme
- Oregano
- Garlic powder
- Onion powder
- Cayenne pepper (adjust to taste)
- Salt
- Black pepper
- 30 ml olive oil

Preparation Instructions:
1. Preheat your Ninja Dual Zone Air Fryer to 200C. This will help get that char on the salmon.
2. In a small bowl, combine the paprika, dried thyme, oregano, garlic powder, onion powder, cayenne pepper, salt, and black pepper to create the Cajun spice blend.
3. Brush both sides of the salmon fillets with olive oil to prevent sticking.
4. Sprinkle the Cajun spice blend generously over both sides of the salmon fillets, pressing it gently so it sticks.
5. Carefully place the seasoned salmon fillets on the non stick plates and into the Air Fryer drawers, skin-side down if they have skin.
6. Cook the salmon for about 3-4 minutes per side, depending on the thickness of the fillets, until the fish is opaque and flakes easily with a fork. The spices should create a dark, flavorful crust on the fish.
7. Once cooked, transfer the Cajun blackened salmon fillets to a serving platter.
8. Serve the salmon hot with a squeeze of fresh lemon juice and garnish with chopped parsley or cilantro, if you would prefer.

Teriyaki Glazed Grilled Salmon

Servings: 2

Prep time: 2 hrs / Cook time: 10 minutes

Ingredients

- 500 grams salmon fillets
- 60 ml soy sauce
- 30 ml mirin (sweet rice wine)
- 30 ml sake (Japanese rice wine)
- 30 ml honey
- 15 ml rice vinegar
- Grated ginger
- 2 cloves garlic, minced
- 15 ml vegetable oil
- Sesame seeds (for garnish)
- Spring onions, sliced (for garnish)

Preparation Instructions:

1. Whisk together the soy sauce, mirin, sake, honey, rice vinegar, grated ginger, and minced garlic to prepare your teriyaki sauce in a bowl.
2. Place the salmon fillets in a shallow dish and pour half the teriyaki sauce. Reserve the remaining sauce for later.
3. Allow the salmon to marinate in the refrigerator for at least 30 minutes, but letting it sit for 1-2 hours allows all flavors to infuse.
4. Preheat your Air Fryer to 2000C
5. Brush the non-stick air Fryer plates with vegetable oil to prevent sticking.
6. Remove the marinated salmon fillets from the dish, allowing any excess marinade to drip off.
7. Place the salmon fillets in the preheated air fryer, skin-side down, and close the lid.
8. Air fry the salmon for about 4-5 minutes per side, basting occasionally with the reserved teriyaki sauce, until the fish is cooked and turns quite brown.
9. While air frying, continue brushing the salmon with the teriyaki sauce to glaze it and enhance the flavor.
10. Once cooked, transfer the teriyaki glazed grilled salmon to a serving platter.
11. Sprinkle sesame seeds and sliced spring onions over the top as a garnish.

Mediterranean Grilled Whole Fish

Servings: 2

Prep time: 10 minutes / Cook time: 10 minutes

Ingredients:

- 1 whole fish (such as sea bass, snapper, or trout), cleaned and scaled (approximately 600-800 grams)
- 30 ml olive oil
- 15 ml lemon juice
- 2 cloves garlic, minced
- Dried oregano
- Dried thyme
- Paprika
- Salt
- Black pepper
- Fresh herbs (such as parsley or basil), for garnish
- Lemon slices (for serving)

Preparation Instructions:

1. Preheat your Air Fryer to 150C.
2. Rinse the whole fish under cold water and pat it dry with paper towels.
3. Mix the olive oil, lemon juice, minced garlic, dried oregano, dried thyme, paprika, salt, and black pepper in a bowl to create the Mediterranean marinade.
4. Make diagonal cuts on both sides of the fish, about 1 inch apart. This will help the marinade penetrate the fish and ensure even cooking.
5. Brush the fish inside and out with the Mediterranean marinade, ensuring it is evenly coated. Reserve a small amount of the marinade for basting during air frying.
6. Place the fish in your preheated Air Fryer drawer, close it, and grill for approximately 4-5 minutes per side, or until the flesh is opaque and flakes easily with a fork.
7. While grilling in your Air fryer, occasionally baste the fish with the reserved marinade to keep it moist and flavorful.
8. Carefully remove the grilled whole fish and transfer it to a serving platter.
9. Serve the Mediterranean grilled whole fish hot, along with a side of roasted vegetables.

Sesame Crusted Ahi Tuna Steaks

Servings: 2

Prep time: 30 minutes / Cook time: 10 minutes

Ingredients
- 2 ahi tuna steaks (150 grams each)
- 30 ml soy sauce
- 15 ml sesame oil
- 15 ml lime juice
- 15 ml honey
- 30 grams sesame seeds
- 2 grams salt
- 2 grams black pepper
- Vegetable oil (for searing)

Preparation Procedures:
1. Combine the soy sauce, sesame oil, lime juice, and honey in a shallow dish to create the marinade.
2. Place the ahi tuna steaks in the marinade and coat them thoroughly. Allow them to marinate in the refrigerator for 30 minutes.
3. Mix the sesame seeds, salt, and black pepper in a separate dish.
4. Remove the tuna steaks from the marinade and gently press them into the sesame seed mixture, ensuring the seeds coat both sides of the steaks.
5. Dab a small amount of vegetable oil on the non stick plates of your Ninja Dual Zone Air Fryer.
6. Sear the sesame crusted tuna steaks for 1-2 minutes per side, or until the sesame seeds are lightly golden and the tuna is rare to medium-rare in the center.
7. Carefully remove the tuna steaks from the Air fryer and let them rest for a few minutes.
8. Slice the sesame crusted ahi tuna steaks into thin strips.
9. Serve them as an appetizer with soy sauce for dipping.

Baja Fish Tacos with Cilantro Lime Sauce

Servings: 2

Prep time: 5 minutes / Cook time: 6 minutes

Ingredients:

For The Fish Tacos:
- 400 grams white fish fillets (such as cod or tilapia)
- 60 grams all-purpose flour
- 5 grams chili powder
- 2 grams garlic powder
- 2 grams cumin
- 2 grams paprika
- 2 grams salt
- 2 grams black pepper
- Vegetable oil (for frying)
- Corn tortillas
- Shredded cabbage or lettuce
- Sliced tomatoes
- Sliced red onions
- Fresh cilantro leaves (for garnish)

For The Cilantro Lime Sauce:
- 120 ml mayonnaise
- 30 ml lime juice
- 15 grams fresh cilantro, chopped
- 1 clove garlic, minced
- Salt and pepper to taste

Preparation Instructions:
1. In a bowl, combine the flour, chili powder, garlic powder, cumin, paprika, salt, and black pepper to make the seasoning mixture for the fish.
2. Pat the fish fillets dry with paper towels and cut them into small strips.
3. Dip each fish strip into the seasoning mixture, coating all sides evenly.
4. Preheat your Ninja Dual Zone Air Fryer to 2000C
5. Carefully place the seasoned fish strips in the preheated Air Fryer and air fry them for 2-3 minutes per side, or until golden brown and crispy.
6. Remove the fried fish from your Ninja Dual Zone Air Fryer and place them on a paper towel-lined plate.
7. To prepare the cilantro lime sauce, combine mayonnaise, lime juice, chopped cilantro, minced garlic, salt, and pepper in a bowl. Mix well until smooth and creamy.
8. Set your Ninja Dual Zone Air Fryer to "Reheat" and warm the corn tortillas in the air fryer for 2-3 minutes or until they are soft and pliable.
9. Assemble the Baja fish tacos by placing some shredded cabbage or lettuce on each tortilla, followed by the crispy fish strips.

10. Top with sliced tomatoes, sliced red onions, and fresh cilantro.

Lemon Herb Baked Cod

Servings: 2
Prep time: 30 minutes / Cook time: 20 minutes

Ingredients:
- 350 grams cod fillets
- 30 ml lemon juice
- 30 ml olive oil
- 2 cloves garlic, minced
- Fresh parsley, chopped
- Fresh dill, chopped
- Dried oregano
- Salt
- Black pepper
- Lemon slices (for garnish)

Preparation Instructions:
1. Preheat your Ninja Dual Zone Air Fryer to 190°C.
2. In a small bowl, whisk together the lemon juice, olive oil, minced garlic, chopped parsley, chopped dill, dried oregano, salt, and black pepper to create the marinade.
3. Place the cod fillets in a baking dish and pour the marinade over them, ensuring they are coated on all sides.
4. Let the cod marinate in the refrigerator for 15-30 minutes to allow the flavors to meld.
5. Once marinated, transfer the baking dish to the preheated Air Fryer and bake for about 15-20 minutes, or until the fish is cooked through. Check with a fork.
6. You can spoon some of the marinade over the cod occasionally to keep it moist and flavorful during baking.
7. Once cooked, remove the lemon herb baked cod from the oven and garnish with lemon slices.
8. Serve the cod hot with steamed vegetables, roasted potatoes, or a side you choose.

Honey Mustard Glazed Salmon

Servings: 2
Prep time: 30 minutes / Cook time: 20 minutes

Ingredients:
- 300 grams salmon fillets
- 45 ml Dijon mustard
- 30 ml honey
- 15 ml soy sauce
- 15 ml lemon juice
- Garlic, minced
- Fresh dill, chopped
- Salt
- Black pepper

Preparation Instructions:
1. Preheat your Air Fryer to 200°C.
2. Whisk together the Dijon mustard, honey, soy sauce, lemon juice, minced garlic, chopped dill, salt, and black pepper to create the honey mustard glaze.
3. Place the salmon fillets in an oven-resistant dish and brush them generously with the honey mustard glaze, ensuring they are evenly coated.
4. Reserve a small amount of the glaze for later use.
5. Let the salmon marinate in the refrigerator for 15-30 minutes to allow the flavors to develop.
6. Once marinated, transfer the baking dish to your preheated Air Fryer and bake for about 12-15 minutes, or until the salmon is cooked through and flakes easily with a fork.
7. While baking, you can brush the salmon with the reserved honey mustard glaze a few times to add extra flavor and glaze.
8. Once cooked, remove the honey mustard glazed salmon from the oven and let it rest for a few minutes.
9. Serve the salmon hot with your favorite sides, such as roasted vegetables.

Lemon Garlic Shrimp Skewers

Servings: 2
Prep time: 30 minutes / Cook time: 20 minutes

Ingredients:
- 300 grams of shrimp, peeled and deveined
- 1 lemon
- 2 cloves of garlic
- 20 ml of olive oil
- Salt and pepper to taste
- Wooden skewers

Preparation Instructions:
1. Soak the wooden skewers in water for about 20

minutes to prevent them from burning in the air dryer.

2. In a mixing bowl, combine the juice of one lemon, minced garlic, olive oil, salt, and pepper. Stir well to make a marinade.

3. Add the shrimp to the marinade and toss to coat them evenly. Let them marinate for at least 15 minutes to allow the flavors to meld.

4. Preheat your Ninja Dual Zone Air Fryer to 170C.

5. Thread the marinated shrimp onto the soaked wooden skewers, dividing them evenly.

6. Place the shrimp skewers in the drawers of your preheated air fryer and cook for about 2-3 minutes per side, or until they turn pink and opaque.

7. While grilling, brush the remaining lemon juice over the shrimp skewers for extra flavor.

8. Remove the skewers from the grill and transfer them to a serving platter.

9. Garnish with freshly chopped parsley and serve hot as an appetizer or main course.

Coconut Shrimp with Sweet Chili Sauce

Servings: 2
Prep time: 30 minutes / Cook time: 20 minutes

Ingredients:
- 500 grams of shrimp, peeled and deveined
- 100 grams of all-purpose flour
- 2 eggs
- 150 grams of shredded coconut
- 30 ml of vegetable oil
- Salt to taste
- Sweet chili sauce for dipping

Preparation Instructions:
1. In three separate bowls, set up a dredging station. Place the flour in the first bowl, beaten eggs in the second bowl, and shredded coconut in the third bowl.

2. Season the shrimp with salt.

3. Dip each shrimp into the flour, shaking off any excess.

4. Then dip the shrimp into the beaten eggs, allowing any excess to drip off.

5. Finally, coat the shrimp with shredded coconut, pressing lightly to ensure it sticks to the shrimp.

6. Place the coated shrimp on a plate or baking sheet and repeat the process with the remaining shrimp.

7. Preheat your Ninja Dual Zone Air Fryer to a temperature of 180C.

8. Once the Air Fryer is preheated, add the coated shrimp in batches, making sure not to overcrowd the airfryer drawer.

9. If you have a lot to Air fry, use both zones in the Air Fryer.

10. Cook for 2-3 minutes per side until the coconut turns golden brown and the shrimp are cooked through.

11. Use a slotted spoon to transfer the cooked shrimp to a paper towel-lined plate to cool much easier.

12. Repeat the cooking process with the remaining shrimp.

13. You can enjoy hot coconut shrimps with sweet chili sauce on the side for dipping.

Garlic Butter Scallops

Servings: 2
Prep time: 30 minutes / Cook time: 20 minutes

Ingredients:
- 300 grams scallops
- Butter
- 2 cloves garlic, minced
- Lemon juice
- Salt, to taste
- Pepper, to taste
- Fresh parsley, chopped (for garnish)

Preparation Instructions:
1. Rinse the scallops under cold water and pat them dry with a paper towel. Season them with salt and pepper on both sides.

2. In your Ninja Dual Zone Air Fryer, melt the butter inside an oven resistant dish at a temperature of 150C. Add the minced garlic and sauté for about 1 minute until fragrant.

3. Carefully place the scallops in the air fryer, making sure not to overcrowd them. Cook for 2-3 minutes on each side until they develop a golden brown crust. Flip them once during cooking.

4. Add the lemon juice to the oven resistant dish and give it a quick stir to coat the scallops. Cook

for 1-2 minutes to allow the flavors to meld together.

5. Remove the dish from the air fryer and transfer the scallops to a serving dish. Drizzle the garlic butter sauce from the skillet over the scallops.

6. Garnish with freshly chopped parsley for added freshness and color. Serve the garlic butter scallops immediately while it's hot .

Bang Bang Shrimp

Servings: 2

Prep time: 30 minutes / Cook time: 20 minutes

Ingredients:
- 250 grams shrimp, peeled and deveined
- 3 tablespoons mayonnaise
- 1 tablespoon sweet chili sauce
- 1 tablespoon Sriracha sauce
- 1 teaspoon honey
- 1 teaspoon lime juice
- 1 clove garlic, minced
- Salt, to taste
- Vegetable oil, for frying
- Green onions, sliced (for garnish)

Preparation Instructions:
1. Combine the mayonnaise, sweet chili sauce, Sriracha sauce, honey, lime juice, minced garlic, and a pinch of salt in a small bowl. Mix well to create the bang bang sauce. Set it aside.

2. Preheat your Ninja Dual Zone Air Fryer to a temperature of 200C. Make sure there is enough oil to fully submerge the shrimp.

3. Rinse the shrimp under cold water and pat them dry with a paper towel. Season them with salt.

4. Lightly spray the air fryer basket with vegetable oil to prevent sticking. Place half of the coated shrimp in one zone of the air fryer basket and the remaining shrimp in the other zone. Make sure they are evenly spaced and not touching each other.

5. Close the air fryer lid and set the timer for 8 minutes. After 4 minutes, open the lid and flip the shrimp to ensure even cooking.

6. Toss the fried shrimp in a large bowl with the prepared bang bang sauce, ensuring each piece is coated evenly.

7. Transfer the bang bang shrimp to a serving plate and garnish with sliced green onions for freshness and presentation.

Crispy Air-Fried Calamari Rings

Servings: 2

Prep time: 30 minutes / Cook time: 20 minutes

Ingredients:
- 250 grams calamari rings
- 100 grams all-purpose flour
- 1 teaspoon paprika
- 1/2 teaspoon garlic powder
- 1/2 teaspoon salt
- 1/4 teaspoon black pepper
- 2 eggs
- Cooking spray or oil (for air frying)
- Lemon wedges (for serving)

Preparation Instructions:
1. Combine the all-purpose flour, paprika, garlic powder, salt, and black pepper in a shallow bowl. Mix well to create the coating mixture.

2. In a separate bowl, beat the eggs until well combined.

3. Dip the calamari rings into the beaten eggs, allow excess eggs drip off, then coat them in the flour mixture, pressing gently to ensure even coating. Repeat the process for all the calamari rings.

4. Preheat the air fryer to 200°C for about 5 minutes.

5. Lightly coat the air fryer drawer with cooking spray or brush it with oil to prevent sticking.

6. Arrange the coated calamari rings in a single layer in the air fryer non stick plates, ensuring they do not overlap.

7. Air fry the calamari rings at 200°C (400°F) for 8-10 minutes, flipping them halfway through, until they turn golden brown and crispy.

8. Once cooked, remove the crispy calamari rings from the air fryer and transfer them to a serving plate. Squeeze fresh lemon juice over the rings and serve.

Spicy Korean BBQ Grilled Shrimp

Servings: 2

Prep time: 120 minutes / Cook time: 6 minutes

Ingredients:

- 300 grams shrimp, peeled and deveined
- 2 tablespoons gochujang (Korean red pepper paste)
- 2 tablespoons soy sauce
- 1 tablespoon honey
- 1 tablespoon sesame oil
- 1 tablespoon rice vinegar
- 2 cloves garlic, minced
- 1 teaspoon grated ginger
- 1/2 teaspoon red pepper flakes (optional for added heat)
- Salt, to taste
- Wooden skewers (pre-soaked in water for grilling)
- Sesame seeds, for garnish
- Chopped green onions, for garnish

Preparation Instructions:

1. In a bowl, combine the gochujang, soy sauce, honey, sesame oil, rice vinegar, minced garlic, grated ginger, red pepper flakes (if using), and a pinch of salt. Mix well to create the marinade.
2. Place the peeled and deveined shrimp in a shallow dish or ziplock bag and pour the marinade over them. Toss the shrimp gently to ensure they are coated evenly. Let them marinate for at least 30 minutes.
3. Marinate them for 1-2 hours in the refrigerator to get the best flavor.
4. Preheat your Ninja Dual Zone Air Fryer to a temperature of 180C.
5. Thread the marinated shrimp onto pre-soaked wooden skewers, piercing through the tail and head ends to keep them secure.
6. Place the shrimp skewers in the preheated Air fryer and cook for 2-3 minutes on each side until they turn opaque and develop grill marks. Baste the shrimp with any remaining marinade during grilling.
7. Remove the grilled shrimp skewers from the air fryer and transfer them to a serving platter.
8. Sprinkle the grilled shrimp with sesame seeds and chopped green onions to add flavor to your dish.

Buffalo-style Air-Fried Shrimp

Servings: 2
Prep time: 120 minutes / Cook time: 6 minutes

Ingredients:

- 500 grams large shrimp, peeled and deveined
- 60 grams all-purpose flour
- 10 grams cornstarch
- 1 teaspoon paprika
- 1/2 teaspoon garlic powder
- 60 ml hot sauce (such as Frank's RedHot
- 1/2 teaspoon salt
- 1/4 teaspoon black pepper
- 2 eggs)
- 60 grams butter, melted
- Cooking spray or oil (for air frying)
- Ranch or blue cheese dressing (for serving)
- Celery sticks (for serving)

Preparation Instructions:

1. Combine the all-purpose flour, cornstarch, paprika, garlic powder, salt, and black pepper in a shallow bowl. Mix well to create the coating mixture.
2. In a separate bowl, beat the eggs. In another bowl, combine the hot sauce and melted butter.
3. Dip the shrimp into the beaten eggs, allowing any excess to drip off, then coat them in the flour mixture, pressing gently to ensure even coating. Repeat the process for all the shrimp.
4. Preheat the Ninja Dual Zone Air Fryer to 200°C (400°F) for about 5 minutes.
5. Lightly coat the air fryer basket with cooking spray or brush it with oil to prevent sticking.
6. Place the coated shrimp in a single layer in the air fryer drawers, ensuring they do not overlap. Set the Dual Zone Air Fryer to Max Crisp mode.
7. Cook the shrimp in the first zone at 200°C (400°F) for 5 minutes.
8. While the first batch is cooking, lightly spray or brush the shrimp in the second zone with oil.
9. Once the first batch is done, transfer the cooked shrimp to a plate and cook the second batch in the second zone at 200°C (400°F) for 5 minutes.
10. Once all the shrimp are cooked, place them in a large bowl and pour the hot sauce and butter mixture over them. Toss the shrimp gently to ensure they are coated evenly.
11. Serve the buffalo-style air-fried shrimp immediately to savor the taste.

Grilled Garlic Butter Lobster Tails

Servings: 2

Prep time: 120 minutes / Cook time: 6 minutes

Ingredients:

- 2 lobster tails
- 60 grams butter, melted
- 2 cloves garlic, minced
- 1 tablespoon fresh lemon juice
- Salt, to taste
- Black pepper, to taste
- Cooking spray or oil (for grilling)
- Fresh parsley, chopped (for garnish)
- Lemon wedges (for serving)

Preparation:

1. Preheat the Ninja Dual Zone Air Fryer to Grill mode.
2. Using kitchen shears or a sharp knife, carefully cut through the top shell of each lobster tail lengthwise, stopping at the tail. Gently spread the shell apart to expose the meat.
3. Combine the melted butter, minced garlic, lemon juice, salt, and black pepper in a small bowl. Mix well to create the garlic butter sauce.
4. Brush the lobster tails generously with the garlic butter sauce, coating the meat thoroughly.
5. Lightly coat the non stick plates of the Ninja Dual Zone Air Fryer with cooking spray or brush it with a little oil to prevent sticking.
6. Place the lobster tails on the non stick plates, meat side down, and close the lid.
7. Grill the lobster tails in the first zone for 4-5 minutes. While the first zone is grilling, preheat the second zone to Grill Mode.
8. After 4-5 minutes, open the lid and flip the lobster tails using tongs or a spatula. Brush the exposed side with more garlic butter sauce.
9. Close the lid and grill the lobster tails in the second zone for 4-5 minutes, or until the meat is opaque and firm.
10. Once grilled to perfection, remove the lobster tails from the Ninja Dual Zone Air Fryer and transfer them to a serving platter.
11. Garnish the lobster tails with freshly chopped parsley for added freshness and presentation.
12. Serve the grilled garlic butter lobster tails

immediately. You can enjoy it with lemon wedges on the side.

Panko-Crusted Air-Fried Shrimp

Servings: 2

Prep time: 120 minutes / Cook time: 6 minutes

Ingredients:

- 500 grams large shrimp, peeled and deveined
- 100 grams all-purpose flour
- 2 eggs, beaten
- 150 grams panko breadcrumbs
- 1 tsp garlic powder
- 1 tsp paprika
- Salt and pepper to taste

Instructions:

1. Preheat the Ninja Dual Zone Air Fryer to 400°F (200°C).
2. Place the flour in a shallow bowl and season with salt and pepper.
3. In another shallow bowl, beat the eggs.
4. Mix the panko breadcrumbs in a third shallow bowl with garlic powder, paprika, salt, and pepper.
5. Dredge the shrimp in the flour, shaking off any excess.
6. Dip the shrimp into the beaten eggs, then coat them in the seasoned panko breadcrumbs, pressing lightly to help the crumbs adhere.
7. Spray the air fryer basket with cooking spray.
8. Arrange the shrimp in a single layer in the basket, ensuring they don't touch each other.
9. Spray the shrimp lightly with cooking spray.
10. Air-fry the shrimp in the Ninja Dual Zone Air Fryer for 6-8 minutes, until golden brown and crispy.
11. Serve immediately with your favorite dipping sauce.

Mediterranean Stuffed Grilled Squid

Servings: 2

Prep time: 5 minutes / Cook time: 8 minutes

Ingredients:

- 4 large squid tubes, cleaned
- 100 grams feta cheese, crumbled

- 50 grams sun-dried tomatoes, chopped
- 50 grams Kalamata olives, chopped
- 50 grams fresh parsley, chopped
- 2 tbsp olive oil
- Salt and pepper to taste

Preparations Instructions:

1. Preheat the Air Fryer to 200°C.
2. Mix the feta cheese, sun-dried tomatoes, Kalamata olives, fresh parsley, olive oil, salt, and pepper in a bowl.
3. Stuff the squid tubes with the feta cheese mixture, leaving about 1 inch of space at the end.
4. Secure the end of each squid tube with a toothpick.
5. Place the stuffed squid tubes in the air fryer basket, ensuring they don't touch each other.
6. Set your Ninja Dual Zone Air Fryer to "AIR FRY", prepare the non stick plates by brushing them with olive oil to avoid sticking.
7. Prepare both zones depending on the sizes of your lobsters and sync the cooking time so they get ready at the same time.
8. Air-fry the squid tubes in the Air Fryer for 6-8 minutes per side, or until the squid is cooked through and the filling is golden brown and crispy.
9. Remove the toothpicks and serve immediately.

Cajun Shrimp and Sausage Foil Packets

Servings: 2
Prep time: 5 minutes / Cook time: 12 minutes

Ingredients:

- 300 grams large shrimp, peeled and deveined
- 200 grams smoked sausage, sliced
- 150 grams bell peppers, sliced
- 150 grams onion, sliced
- 2 cloves garlic, minced
- 30 grams Cajun seasoning
- 30 ml olive oil
- Salt and pepper, to taste
- Fresh parsley, chopped (for garnish)

Preparation Instructions:

1. Preheat your Air Fryer to 200°C.
2. Combine the shrimp, sausage, bell peppers, onion, minced garlic, Cajun seasoning, olive oil, salt, and pepper in a large bowl. Toss well to

coat the Ingredients evenly.
3. Divide the mixture into two equal portions and place each portion on a sheet of aluminum foil. Fold the foil over the Ingredients, sealing the edges to create a packet.
4. Place the foil packets in the Ninja Dual Zone Air Fryer. Cook for 10-12 minutes or until the shrimp is cooked and the sausage is heated.
5. Carefully remove the foil packets from the air fryer and let them cool slightly before opening.
6. Sprinkle fresh parsley on top for garnish.
7. Serve the Cajun shrimp and sausage foil packets as a delicious and flavorful meal. You can enjoy them as they are or serve with rice or crusty bread.

Chimichurri Grilled Shrimp

Servings: 2
Prep time: 5 minutes / Cook time: 12 minutes

Ingredients:

- 400 g large shrimp, peeled and deveined
- 60 ml olive oil
- 30 ml red wine vinegar
- 15 g fresh parsley, finely chopped
- 15 g fresh cilantro, finely chopped
- 2 cloves garlic, minced
- 1 tablespoon lemon juice
- 1 teaspoon dried oregano
- 1/2 teaspoon red pepper flakes (adjust to taste)
- Salt and pepper, to taste
- Lemon wedges (for serving)

Preparation Instructions:

1. Preheat your Ninja Dual Zone Air Fryer to 200°C.
2. Combine the olive oil, red wine vinegar, chopped parsley, chopped cilantro, minced garlic, lemon juice, dried oregano, red pepper flakes, salt, and pepper in a bowl. Mix well to make the chimichurri marinade.
3. Add the shrimp to the marinade and toss to coat them evenly. Let the shrimp marinate for about 15 minutes to allow the flavors to infuse.
4. Once marinated, put the shrimp onto skewers, leaving a small space between each shrimp.
5. Place the shrimp skewers in the Ninja Dual Zone Air Fryer. Cook for 5-6 minutes, turning halfway through, or until the shrimp are cooked and

slightly charred.

6. Remove the shrimp skewers from the air fryer and let them rest for a few minutes.

7. Serve the chimichurri grilled shrimp with lemon wedges on the side.

Well-Baked Spicy Salmon with A Drizzle Of Chilli Sauce

Prep time: 7 minutes | Cook time: 15 minutes | Serves 4 .

Ingredients:

- 130g x 4 Salmon fillets
- 420g peas
- 1 tbsp curry powder
- 1 tsp cumin seeds
- 20ml lemon juice
- 30g crème fraîche
- 30ml milk
- ¼ tsp black pepper, grounded
- 1cal olive fry spray
- 60g of medium chilli sauce

Preparation Instructions:

1. Employing a medium sized bowl, amalgamate curry powder, cumin seeds and lemon to make a spicy paste for the salmon

2. Using this paste, cover both sides of each salmon fillet

3. Spray the salmon thoroughly, using the 1cal fry

4. Place the salmon in the zone 1 draw and peas in the zone 2 draw

5. Select zone 1 using the 'bake' function at 180°C for 10 minutes, and zone 2 with 'dehydrate' at 40°C for 7 minutes

6. Select 'SYNC' followed by 'START/STOP' to initiate the cooking process

7. Flip the salmon half way through cooking at 5 minutes

8. Retrieve the salmon and plate them up

9. Remove the peas then mash them up in a large bowl using a masher

10. Add crème fraîche and milk to the peas, then stir with a fork to make a putée

11. Evenly dollop the pea purée on the plate to accompany the salmon

12. To finalise, drizzle 1 tbsp of chilli sauce over each portion of salmon then serve

Masala Salmon Bites Served with Concentrated Mint Chutney

Prep time: 10 minutes | Cook time: 10 minutes| Serves 4

Ingredients:
For Salmon
- 500g salmon fillets (125g x 4)
- 2 tsp sea salt
- 1 ½ tsp turmeric Powder
- 1 ½ tsp coriander
- 2 tsp tandoori

For Chutney
- 80g coriander, diced
- 1 green chilli, diced
- 1 garlic clove, diced
- 4 tomatoes, diced
- ½ tsb chilli flakes
- ½ tsp Himalayan salt

Preparation Instructions:

1. Place all of the spice powders into a small bowl

2. Rub the spice mix onto the salmon thoroughly

3. Place 2 fillets in each ninja foodi draw

4. Select 'AIR FRY' at 200°C for 10 minutes

5. Press 'MATCH' then 'START/STOP to initiate air frying the fish

6. Flip the salmon half way through the cooking duration

7. During the next 5 minutes, prepare the mint sauce by grinding 'for chutney' Ingredients, accept the salt and chilli flakes

8. Add salt and chilli flakes, then combine using a fork and pour the chutney into a pot

9. Retrieve the masala salmon chop each fillet into 4 chunks (4x4 = 16 bites)

10. Place the masala salmon bites into a large dish with a pot of concentrated chutney in the centre to serve

Air Fried Calamari & Lime Wedges

Prep time: 1 minutes | Cook time: 12 minutes| Serves 8

Ingredients:
- 680g calamari (squid rings)
- 2 limes
- 1cal olive fry spray

Preparation Instructions:

1. Preheat the ninja foodi to 200°C for 5 minutes
2. Place 4 servings of calamari (340g) into each zone draw of the ninja foodi
3. Select the zone setting and pair it with 'AIR FRY' at 200°C for 12 minutes
4. Press 'MATCH' followed by 'STOP/START' to defrost and cook calamari
5. Meanwhile, cut 2 limes into 8 quarters
6. Shake the calamari at the 5 minute mark of cooking
7. Retrieve the food content and divide it amongst 8 plates
8. Place a lime wedges on top of each portion of calamari

Scottish Smoked Salmon Bake

Prep time: 6 minutes | Cook time: 15 minutes | Serves 4

Ingredients:

- 250g smoked salmon chunks
- 80g smoked salmon shavings
- 100g soft cheese
- 4 eggs, beaten
- 220ml milk
- 20g fresh parsley, chopped
- 20g chives, finely diced
- 10g spring onions, finely diced
- 1/8 tsp ground pepper
- 1Cal olive fry spray

Preparation Instructions:

1. Preheat the dual zone to 180°C for 5 minutes
2. Spray two 4" bake pots, then place the salmon chunks in
3. Employing another medium sized bowl, toss in soft cheese and beat it with a fork
4. Add egg and milk to form a mixture, then top with chives, parsley, and spring onions
5. Toss this newly formed mixture on top of the salmon chunks
6. Top the pots with the salmon shavings
7. Place the baking pots in the draws of the dual zone and pairing them to 'BAKE' at 180°C for 15 minutes
8. Retrieve the fish bake, divide each bake pot into 2 servings

Rolled Fishcakes With 'Saucy Sauce' Dip

Prep time: 10 minutes | Cook time: 10-12 minutes| Serves 4

Ingredients:
For rolled fish cake

- 300g cuttlefish, finely chopped
- 15g finely chopped coriander
- 30g mayonnaise
- 2 tbsp sweet chilli sauce
- 80g of dried breadcrumbs
- 1 large egg
- 1/8 tsp sea salt
- ½ tsp ground pepper
- 1cal olive oil fry spray
- 400g canned green beans, halved

For sauce

- 75g tomato ketchup
- 75g mayonnaise

Preparation Instructions:

1. Spay the duel zone draws generously, using 1cal fry spray
2. Preheat the duel zone at 200°C for 4-5 minutes
3. Using a mixing bowl, amalgamate the fish, coriander, egg, mayo, and sweet chilli sauce by hand mixing
4. Hand shape the mixture into 4 rolled fishcakes
5. Place the 2 rolled fishcake in each zone draw of the dual zone
6. Pair the zone draws to 'AIR FRY' at 200° for 10 minutes
7. Press 'MATCH' followed by 'START/STOP' to cook the contents
8. Meanwhile, in a mixing bowl, stir together the ketchup and mayonnaise to form a pink coloured sauce
9. Flip the rolled fish cakes at the 5 minute mark of cooking
10. Retrieve the food content plate up the rolled fishcakes with a heap of sauce per serving

Coated Tilapia

Prep time: 20 minutes | Cook time: 8 minutes | Serves 4
Baked lemon sole fillets, coated with cheesy breadcrumbs.

Ingredients:

- 4 x 120g tilapia fillets
- 30g all-purpose flour
- 60g panko bread crumbs
- 30g parmesan cheese, grated
- 1 large egg, beaten
- 1cal olive fry spray
- ¼ tsp sea salt
- ¼ tsp black pepper, grounded

Preparation Instructions:

1. Preheat the dual zone to 180°C for 5 minutes
2. Using a small bowl, combine the flour and seasoning
3. Rub this powder mixture over the tilapia filets
4. Employing another small bowl, amalgamate parmesan and panko breadcrumbs with a fork
5. Submerge the tilapia fillets in the egg and then bread crumb mixture
6. To finalise the tilapia fillets, spray the them thoroughly with the 1cal olive
7. Place 2 tilapia fillers in each zone draw of the dual zone
8. Pair the zone draws to 'BAKE' at 180°C for 8 minutes
9. Press 'MATCH' followed by 'START/STOP' to cook the tilapia
10. Flip the tilapia fillets half way through the cooking process
11. Retrieve the coated tilapia fillets and serve

Garlicky Tiger Prawns with Aubergine

Prep time: 10 minutes / Cook time: 16 minutes
Serves 4

Ingredients:

- 12 tiger prawns, peeled, tails on
- 1 tbsp butter, melted
- Juice of 1 lemon
- 1 tbsp stone-ground mustard
- 2 garlic cloves, pressed
- 1 tsp dried parsley flakes
- Sea salt and ground black pepper, to taste
- 1 tbsp olive oil

500g aubergine, cut in 2.5cm pieces

Preparation Instructions:

1. Insert crisper plates in both drawers. Spray the crisper plates with nonstick cooking oil.
2. Toss tiger prawns with butter, lemon juice, mustard, garlic, parsley, salt, and black pepper.
3. Toss aubergine pieces with salt and black pepper. Drizzle them with olive oil.
4. Place the prawns in the zone 1 drawer and the aubergine pieces in the zone 2 drawer.
5. Select zone 1 and pair it with "AIR FRY" at 200°C for 9 to 10 minutes. Select zone 2 and pair it with "AIR FRY" at 190°C for 15 to 16 minutes. Select "SYNC" followed by the "START/STOP" button.
6. When zone 1 time reaches 5 minutes, turn the prawns over using silicone-tipped tongs.
7. When zone 2 time reaches 8 minutes, shake the drawer and reinsert it to continue cooking.

One-Pan Seafood Pilau

Prep time: 10 minutes / Cook time: 15 minutes
Serves 4

Ingredients:

- 300g white fish, skinless, boneless and cut into strips
- 300g shrimp, cleaned and deveined
- 1 tbsp olive oil
- 2 bell peppers, deveined and chopped
- 200ml vegetable broth
- 1 (400g) can tomatoes, chopped
- 1 onion, chopped
- 2 garlic cloves, crushed or finely chopped
- 2 ancho chiles, chopped
- 2 tbsp olive oil
- 400g cooked rice
- 100g frozen sweet corn kernels, thawed

Preparation Instructions:

1. Mix the Ingredients until everything is well combined. Divide the mixture between two baking tins. Add baking tins to the drawers.
2. Select zone 1 and pair it with "ROAST" at 190°C for 15 minutes. Select "MATCH" to duplicate settings across both zones. Press the "START/STOP" button.
3. At the halfway point, stir your pilau with a wooden spoon and reinsert the drawers to resume cooking.
4. Allow your pilau to sit for about 10 minutes before serving. Devour!

Chapter 5: Snacks and Appetizer Recipes

Crispy Zucchini Fries

Servings: 2
Prep time: 5 minutes / Cook time: 15 minutes

Ingredients:
- 2 medium zucchinis
- 115g breadcrumbs
- 50g grated Parmesan cheese
- 1 teaspoon garlic powder
- 1/2 teaspoon paprika
- Salt and pepper to taste
- 2 eggs, beaten

Preparation Instructions:
1. Preheat your Air Fryer to 200°C.
2. Cut the zucchinis into thin strips that look like fries.
3. Combine the breadcrumbs, Parmesan cheese, garlic powder, paprika, salt, and pepper in a shallow dish.
4. Dip each zucchini strip into the bowl that has the beaten eggs, then move it into the bowl with the breadcrumb mixture to coat it.
5. Place the coated zucchini fries on the non stick plates of the air fryer drawer.
6. Air fry in the air fryer for 10-12 minutes or until the fries are golden brown and crispy.
7. Remove from the air fryer and serve while it's hot with any dipping sauce of your choice.

Bacon-Wrapped Jalapeño Poppers

Servings: 2
Prep time: 5 minutes / Cook time: 15 minutes

Ingredients:
- 12 jalapeño peppers
- 230g cream cheese, softened
- 12 slices bacon, cut in half

Preparation Instructions:
1. Preheat your Ninja Dual Zone Air Fryer to 190°C.
2. Cut each jalapeño pepper in half lengthwise and remove the seeds.
3. Fill each jalapeño half with cream cheese, using about 1 tablespoon per pepper.
4. Wrap each filled jalapeño half with a slice of bacon, securing with a toothpick if needed.
5. Place the bacon-wrapped jalapeño poppers in the air fryer drawer.
6. Set the Zone 1 in your Ninja Dual Zone Air Fryer to "AIR FRY" and cook in the air fryer for 12-15 minutes or until the bacon is crispy.
7. Carefully remove from the air fryer and let it cool slightly before serving.

Buffalo Cauliflower Bites

Servings: 2
Prep time: 5 minutes / Cook time: 18 minutes

Ingredients:
- 1 medium head of cauliflower, cut into bite-sized florets
- Hot sauce
- 2 tablespoons melted butter
- 1 teaspoon garlic powder
- 1/2 teaspoon paprika
- Salt and pepper to taste

Preparation Instructions:
1. Preheat your Ninja Dual Zone Air Fryer to 190°C.
2. Whisk together the hot sauce, melted butter, garlic powder, paprika, salt, and pepper in a bowl.
3. Add the cauliflower florets to the bowl and toss until they are well coated in the buffalo sauce mixture.
4. Place the cauliflower florets in the air fryer drawer.
5. Set your Ninja Dual Zone Air Fryer to the "AIR FRY" option.
6. Cook the cauliflower florets in the air fryer for 15-18 minutes. Toss it when it's halfway through, and cook until the cauliflower is crispy and golden.
7. Remove from the air fryer and serve hot with ranch or blue cheese dressing for dipping.

Mini Chicken Satay Skewers

Servings: 2
Prep time: 7 minutes / Cook time: 12 minutes

Ingredients
- 450g boneless chicken breast, cut into small pieces
- 3 tablespoons soy sauce
- 2 tablespoons peanut butter
- 1 tablespoon lime juice
- 1 teaspoon curry powder
- 1/2 teaspoon garlic powder
- Wooden skewers, soaked in water

Preparation Instructions:
1. Preheat your Ninja Dual Zone Air Fryer to 190°C.
2. To make the marinade, take out a bowl and whisk together the soy sauce, peanut butter, lime juice, curry powder, and garlic powder.
3. Thread the chicken pieces onto the soaked wooden skewers.
4. Place the chicken skewers in a shallow dish and pour the marinade over them, ensuring they are evenly coated.
5. Transfer the skewers to the air fryer drawers.
6. Cook the skewers in the air fryer for 10-12 minutes, or until the chicken is cooked enough to your liking and slightly charred.
7. Remove from the air fryer and serve hot with your favorite dipping sauce.

Mozzarella Sticks

Servings: 2
Prep time: 3 minutes / Cook time: 8 minutes

Ingredients:
- 8 mozzarella cheese sticks
- 120g breadcrumbs or panko
- 1 teaspoon Italian seasoning
- 1/2 teaspoon garlic powder
- 2 eggs, beaten

Preparation Instructions:
1. Preheat your Ninja Dual Zone Air Fryer to 190°C.
2. Combine the breadcrumbs or panko, Italian seasoning, and garlic powder in a shallow dish.
3. Dip each mozzarella stick into the beaten eggs, then dip into the bowl with the breadcrumb mixture.
4. Place the coated mozzarella sticks in the air fryer

drawer.
5. Cook in the air fryer for 6-8 minutes until the cheese is melted and the coating is golden and crispy.
6. Remove from the air fryer and let cool for a few minutes before serving with marinara sauce or your favorite dip.

Sweet Potato Fries

Servings: 2
Prep time: 7 minutes / Cook time: 15 minutes

Ingredients:
- 2 medium sweet potatoes, cut into thin strips
- 2 tablespoons olive oil
- 1 teaspoon paprika
- 1/2 teaspoon garlic powder
- Salt and pepper to taste

Preparation Instructions:
1. Preheat your Ninja Dual Zone Air Fryer to 200°C.
2. Toss the sweet potato strips with olive oil, paprika, garlic powder, salt, and pepper until well coated in a bowl.
3. Place the sweet potato strips in the air fryer drawer in a single layer.
4. Cook in the air fryer for 12-15 minutes, or until the sweet potato fries are crispy and golden brown, shaking the basket halfway through to ensure even cooking.
5. Remove from the air fryer and serve hot with your favorite dipping sauce.

Coconut Shrimp

Servings: 2
Prep time: 6 mins / Cook time: 10 minutes

Ingredients:
- 450g peeled and deveined shrimp
- 2 eggs, beaten
- 80 g shredded coconut

Instructions:
1. Preheat your Ninja Dual Zone Air Fryer to 190°C.
2. Dip each shrimp in the beaten eggs, and coat with the shredded coconut.
3. Place the coated shrimp in the air fryer drawer lining it with some parchment paper to help with cleaning. Alternatively, you can place the coated

shrimp on the non stick plates and in the Air Fryer drawers.

4. Cook in the air fryer for 8-10 minutes or until the shrimp are cooked, and the coconut is golden and crispy.

5. Remove from the air fryer and serve hot with any dipping sauce.

Mini Spinach and Feta Quiches

Servings: 2

Prep time: 5 minutes / Cook time: 12 minutes

Ingredients:

- 4 large eggs
- 60ml milk
- 30g chopped spinach
- 113g crumbled feta cheese
- Salt and pepper to taste

Preparation Instructions:

1. Preheat your Air Fryer to 190°C.
2. In a bowl, whisk together the eggs and milk. Season with salt and pepper.
3. Divide the chopped spinach and crumbled feta cheese evenly among greased muffin cups.
4. Pour the egg mixture over the spinach and feta in each muffin cup, filling about 3/4 full.
5. Place the muffin cups in the air fryer drawer.
6. Cook in the air fryer for 10-12 minutes, or until the quiches are set and lightly golden.
7. Remove from the air fryer and let cool for a few minutes before serving.

Stuffed Mushrooms

Servings: 2

Prep time: 5 minutes / Cook time: 12 minutes

Ingredients:

- 12 large mushrooms
- 115g breadcrumbs
- 50g grated Parmesan cheese
- 2 cloves garlic, minced
- 2 tablespoons chopped fresh parsley
- Salt and pepper to taste

Preparation Instructions:

1. Preheat your Ninja Dual Zone Air Fryer to 190°C.
2. Remove the stems from the mushrooms and set aside.

Place the mushroom caps in the air fryer drawer.

3. Combine the breadcrumbs, Parmesan cheese, minced garlic, chopped parsley, salt, and pepper in a bowl.
4. Finely chop the reserved mushroom stems and add them to the breadcrumb mixture. Stir to combine.
5. Fill each mushroom cap with the breadcrumb mixture, pressing gently to compact it.
6. Place the stuffed mushrooms in the air fryer drawer.
7. Cook in the air fryer for 10-12 minutes until the mushrooms are tender and the topping is golden.
8. Remove from the air fryer and serve hot.

Mini Rump Steaks & Raw Thyme

Servings: 12

Prep time: 10 minutes / Cook time: 10 minutes

Ingredients:
Steak

- Rump steak (50g x 12)
- 1 tbsp olive oil
- ¼ tsp Himalayan salt
- ¼ tsp ground black pepper
- 1 tbsp unsalted butter
- 1 crushed garlic clove
- 1 ¼ tbsp rosemary

For thyme

- 6 fresh thyme stalks

Preparation Instructions:

1. Combine the Ingredients by rubbing them into the meat and allow 1hr for the flavours to infuse
2. Preheat the ninja foodi at 180°C for 4-5 minutes
3. Place the meats inside 6 Steak pieces in each ninja zone
4. Select ninja zone and pair them with 'ROAST' at 180°C for 7 minutes
5. Press 'MATCH' followed by 'START/STOP' to cook the steaks
6. Meanwhile cut the thyme stalks in half to create 12 pieces
7. Retrieve the steaks, plate them up, then place half a thyme stalk on top to serve

Juicy Beef Sliders

Servings: 16

Prep time: 20 minutes / Cook time: 8 minutes

Ingredients:
Mini Burgers
- 600g Beef mince
- 10g chopped coriander
- 1 large egg yolk
- 1 tbsp olive oil
- ¼ tsp of sea salt
- ¼ tsp of ground black pepper
- 1 tbsp dijon mustard

To serve/condiments
- 16 quarter slices of British mature cheddar
- 16 quarter sliced beef tomato
- 16 tsp of tomato ketchup or BBQ sauce
- ½ shredded lettuce
- 16 mini wholemeal buns, sliced vertically

Preparation Instructions:
1. Mix all of the 'mini burgers' Ingredients in a mixing bowl and shape them up into 16 mini burger patties (quarter the size of your palm)
2. Preheat the air fryer at 180°C for 4-5 minutes
3. Place the mini burger patties in zone 1 of the ninja foodi and the mini burger buns in zone 2
4. Select zone 1 and pair it with 'BAKE' at 180°C for 8 minutes
5. Select zone 2 and pair it with 'ROAST at 140°C for 2 minutes
6. Press 'SYNC' followed by 'START/STOP' to cook the food content
7. Flip the burgers at the 6 minute mark, just around the time the buns will start heating up
8. Retrieve the food content, place the bottom layers of the buns on a dish
9. In order, top the bun with lettuce, sliced tomato, burger patty, cheese, 1 tsp of preferred sauce
10. Place the top layers of the buns on the burger
11. Penetrate mini wooden flat paddle in the centre of the burger to help hold it together

Mini Hot Dogs Rolls

Servings: 8
Prep time: 1 minutes / Cook time: 20 minutes

Ingredients:
- 15 frozen mini hot dog rolls
- 1cal olive fry spray
- Dipping sauce of choice

Preparation Instructions
1. Preheat the ninja foodi to 180°C for 5 minutes
2. Place 8 rolls in zone 1 and 7 rolls in zone 2
3. Select zone 1 and pair it with 'BAKE' at 180°C for 12 minutes
4. Select zone 2 and pair it with 'BAKE' at 180°C for 11 minutes
5. Press 'SYNC' followed by 'STOP/START' to defrost and cook the mini sausage rolls
6. Shake the sausage rolls at the 5 minute mark of cooking
7. Retrieve the food content and place it on a large dish to serve with a dipping sauce of choice

Breaded Air Fried Celery With 'Thousand Island' Dressing

Servings: 8
Prep time: 5 minutes / Cook time: 8 minutes

Ingredients:
- 20 medium celery sticks
- 130g panko bread crumbs
- 65g all-purpose flour
- 1 large egg
- ½ tablespoon water
- 30g all-purpose flour
- ½ teaspoon garlic powder
- ½ teaspoon paprika
- ½ teaspoon dried dill
- 120g 'thousand Island' dressing
- 1Cal olive oil fry spray

Preparation Instructions
1. With the crisper plates, preheat the ninja foodi to 200°C for 4-5 minutes
2. Cut the celery stalks in half to create 40 pieces
3. Employ 3 large bowls, add bread crumbs in #1, egg/water in #2 and combine flour, garlic powder, paprika, and dill in #3
4. Submerge the celery sticks in the flour spice, egg and then panko bread crumbs to coat
5. Spray the zone draws then toss in the coated celery sticks (20 in each draw). Select the zones and pair them to 'AIR FRY' at 200°C for 8 minutes
6. Flip the breaded celery sticks at the 4 minute mark of air frying, then leave them for another 4 minutes
7. Retrieve the celery sticks, place them on a large dish,

cover with the 'thousand island' dressing to serve

Nachos & Cheese

Servings: 2
Prep time: 5 minutes / Cook time: 8 minutes

Ingredients:
For Nachos
- 8 6-inch corn tortillas
- 2 tbsp avocado oil
- ½ teaspoon kosher salt

For Cheese topping
- 60g butter
- 60g all purpose flour
- 400ml milk
- 400g grated cheddar cheese
- 1 tsp sea salt

Preparation Instructions:
1. Drizzle the oil and salt on the tortillas
2. Cut the tortilla into 8 triangle like slices
3. Place the Nachos in the zone 1 draw
4. Toss the 'for cheese topping' Ingredients in the zone 2 draw
5. Select zone 1, pairing it with the 'BAKE' function at 180°C for 5 minutes
6. Select zone 2, pairing it with 'ROAST' at 140°C for 5 minutes
7. To cook the content press 'SYNC' and 'START/STOP'
8. Pull the draw out and shake the Nachos at the 3 minute mark of cooking
9. Stir the cheese topping at the and then the zone 2 eeherature up to 180°C and cook for another 4 minutes
10. Retrieve the Nachos and place them in a share bowl, then into a cheese, then top with the cheese topping to serve

Chinese Spring Rolls With Sweet Chilli Sauce

Servings: 16
Prep time: 40 minutes / Cook time: 12 minutes

Ingredients:
- 16 sprint roll wrappers
- 2 medium eggs
- 1 tbsp sesame seed oil
- 1cal olive fry spray

- 1 garlic clove, minced
- 350g cabbage, diced
- 300g carrots, chopped into thin sticks
- 200g mushrooms
- 60ml lime juice
- 1 tbsp fish sauce
- 1 tbsp soy sauce
- 1 tbsp corm starch

To serve
- 250ml sweet chilli sauce

Preparation Instructions:
1. Preheat the dual zone to 200°C for 6 minutes
2. On a large sauce pan and stove, heat up the oil at medium heat, then dash in the garlic mince
3. Toss the vegetables into the sauce pan and cook them until they become soft
4. Turn off the heat then pour in the fish and soy sauce, then combine with a wooden spoon
5. Dollop some mixture into each spring roll wrapper, fold them tightly and seal the ends
6. In a medium bowl, stir egg and corn starch into a paste
7. Rub this newly formed past into the spring rolls
8. Place 8 spring rolls in each zone draw of the air fryer, then spray them with 1cal olive
9. Pair both of the zone draws with 'AIR FRY' at 200°C for 6 minutes
10. Press 'MATCH' then 'START/STOP' to begin air frying the spring rolls
11. At the 3 minute mark flip the spring rolls
12. At the end of the cooking duration, retrieve the spring rolls and plate them up with 1 heaped tbsp of sweet chilli sauce to serve

Sesame Feta Cheese & Cherry Tomato Bites

Servings: 4
Prep time: 8 minutes / Cook time: 8 minutes

Ingredients:
For sesame feta cheese
- 450g feta cheese block
- 4 tbsp white sesame seeds
- 4 tbsp black sesame seeds
- 1 large egg

For cherry tomatoes
- 800g cheery tomatoes, on branches

- ½ tsp sea salt
- ½ tsp garlic, grounded
- ½ tap black pepper, grounded
- 2 tbsp olive oil

Preparation Instructions:
1. Preheat the dual zone to 180°C for 4 minutes
2. Using a kitchen knife, cut 12 equally sized feta cheese cubes
3. Beat an egg in a bowl and dunk in the feta cheese
4. Using a small pot, stick together sesame seeds and the egg covered feta cheese, then place them in the zone 1 draw of the dual zone
5. Hand combine the 'for cherry tomato' Ingredients and place them in the zone 2 draw of the dual zone
6. Pair both zones to 'ROAST' at 180°C for 8 minutes
7. Press 'MATCH' followed by 'STOP/START' to roast the cheese and tomato
8. At the 4 minute mark of cooking give both food content a shake
9. Retrieve the food contents and pierce them on small wooden paddles to serve

Goat Cheese Balls With Honey

Servings: 4
Prep time: 10 minutes / Cook time: 8 minutes

Ingredients:
- 280g goats cheese
- 40g all-purpose flour
- 1 large egg
- 135g crushed corn flakes
- 30ml lemon juice
- 1 tbsp honey
- 1Cal fry spray

Preparation Instructions:
1. Spray the zone draws if the air fryer, insert the crisper plates and then preheat it zone to 180°C for 4 minutes
2. Roll up the goats cheese into small balls
3. Beat the eggs and lemon into a small bowl, add cornflakes in second bowl, and flour in a third bowl
4. Dunk the cheese balls in flour, egg, then cornflakes
5. Divide the balls amongst both zone draws of the air fryer
6. Pair the zone draws to 'AIR FRY' at 180°C for 8 minutes
7. Press 'MATCH' followed by 'START/STOP' to begin the air frying process

8. At the 4 minute mark if air frying, flip the goat cheese balls.
9. Once complete, retrieve the goat cheese balls and drizzle with honey

Crispy Crab Chips

Servings: 8
Prep time: 5 minutes / Cook time: 15 minutes

Ingredients:
- 350g crab sticks
- ½ tsp sea salt
- ½ tsp black pepper, grounded
- 1cal olive spray

Preparation Instructions:
1. Preheat the dual zone to 170°C for 5 minutes
2. Meanwhile, using a large mixing bowl combine salt, pepper, and oil
3. Add the crab sticks to this seasoning
4. Toss the crab sticks in both zone draws, then pair them to 'AIR FRY' at 160°C for 15 minutes
5. Press 'MATCH' followed by 'START/STOP' to cook the crab sticks
6. At the 7 minute mark of cooking, give the crab sticks a shake
7. Once done, retrieve the crab sticks and serve between 8

Autumn Air Roasted Pumpkin Seeds

Serves 4
Servings: 4
Prep time: 3 minutes / Cook time: 15 minutes

Ingredients
- 120g Pumpkin seeds
- 30g butter
- ¼ tsp sea salt
- ¼ tsp black pepper, grounded

Preparation Instructions
1. Preheat the ninja foodi unit to 200°C for 5 minutes
2. Meanwhile, mix the butter salt and pepper with the Pumpkin seeds
3. Toss 60g of Pumpkin seeds in each zone draw, then pair them to 'ROAST' at 180°C for 15 minutes.
4. Press 'MATCH' followed by 'STOP/START' Christmas pork

5. At the 8-minute mark of cooking, pull out the zone draw and give the pumpkin seeds a shake
6. At the end of the cooking duration, retrieve the roasted Pumpkin seeds and place them in a share bowl

Air Fried Spicy Pumpkin Seeds

Servings: 8
Prep time: 15 minutes / Cook time: 12 minutes

Ingredients
- 240g pumpkin seeds, dried
- 2 tsp ghee, melted
- ½ tsp chilli powder
- 1/8 tsp chilli flakes
- ½ tsp sea salt
- 1 tsp black pepper, grounded

Preparation Instructions
1. Preheat the dual zone to 170°C for 5 minutes
2. Meanwhile, toss the pumpkin seeds in a large mixing bowl and pour in butter, chilli products, salt, and pepper
3. Divide the seeds into both draws of the dual zone
4. Pair the zone draws with 'ROAST' at 170°C for 12 minutes
5. Give the zone draws a shake at the 6-minute mark of cooking
6. Once done, remove the seeds and serve

Sweet Popcorn Drizzled With Toffee Sauce

Servings: 4-5
Prep time: 30minutes / Cook time: 21 minutes

Ingredients
- 100g raw popcorn kernels
- 1 cal olive oil spray
- 1 tbs sugar
- 75ml Toffee sauce, premade

Preparation Instructions
1. Line both zone draws with the crisper plates
2. Place 50g of kernels in each zone draw
3. Spray the kernels with olive oil and dash and sugar in
4. Select the zones, pairing with 'AIR FRY' at 200°C for 15 minutes
5. Press 'MATCH' then 'START/STOP' to begin

popping the kernels
6. Give the draws a shake at the 7-minute mark of air frying, but keep well away to ensure the corn does not pop into your face
7. Retrieve the popcorn, and then pile it up into a share bowl sprinkle then drizzle with toffee sauce

Halloumi Popcorn

Servings: 4
Prep time: 20minutes / Cook time: 10 minutes

Ingredients
- 2 teaspoons of smoked paprika
- 1 teaspoon of brown sugar
- 1 teaspoon of mustard powder
- 1 teaspoon of cornflour
- 1 teaspoon of onion powder
- 1/2 teaspoon of garlic powder
- 225g halloumi, cubed
- 2 eggs
- 60g breadcrumbs

Preparation Instructions
1. Preheat your air fryer to 180 degrees Celsius.
2. Mix together the paprika, sugar, mustard powder, corn flour, onion powder and garlic powder in a dish.
3. Add the halloumi and coat each piece gently.
4. Beat the eggs and dip each piece of halloumi into the egg then the breadcrumbs.
5. Place the halloumi into the air fryer and fry for 8 to 10 minutes or until golden brown.

Mozzarella Chips

Servings: 8 pieces
Prep time: 20 minutes / Cook time: 5 minutes

Ingredients
- 2 tablespoons of white flour
- 3 teaspoons of garlic powder
- 2 large eggs
- 150g breadcrumbs
- 550 g mozzarella in a block

Preparation Instructions
1. Mix flour and garlic powder in one bowl.
2. In another bowl whisk the eggs.
3. Place breadcrumbs in a third bowl.
4. Slice mozzarella into 2 cm thick strips.

5. Dip the mozzarella into the flour, then the egg and finally the breadcrumbs.
6. Spray air fryer tray and mozzarella sticks with non stick cooking spray.
7. Air fry for 4 to 5 minutes in batches at 180 degrees Celsius.

The Best Pigs-in-Blankets Ever

Servings: 6
Prep time: 10 minutes / Cook time: 15 minutes

Ingredients
- 12 cocktail sausages, casing removed
- 6 rashers pancetta, cut into halves lengthwise
- 1 tsp hot paprika

Preparation Instructions
1. Insert crisper plates in both drawers. Spray the crisper plates with nonstick cooking oil.
2. Wrap sausages in the pancetta slices and arrange them in both drawers in your Ninja Foodi.
3. Select zone 1 and pair it with "AIR FRY" at 180°C for 15 minutes. Select "MATCH" followed by the "START/STOP" button.
4. At the halfway point, turn the pigs-in-blankets over, and reinsert the drawers to resume cooking.
5. Sprinkle warm pigs-in-blankets with hot paprika and enjoy!

The Best Wings Ever

Servings: 4
Prep time: 8 minutes / Cook time: 33 minutes

Ingredients
- 1 kg chicken wings, drumettes & flats
- 1 tbsp butter, melted
- 1/2 tsp ground cumin
- 1 tsp garlic powder
- 2 tbsp Worcestershire sauce
- 1 tsp hot paprika
- 2 tbsp golden syrup
- Sea salt and ground black pepper, to taste

Preparation Instructions
1. Place all the Ingredients in a ceramic bowl. Give them a good stir, cover the bowl, and let the chicken wings marinate for approximately 1 hour in the fridge.
2. Drain and reserve the marinade.

3. Insert crisper plates in both drawers. Spray the crisper plates with nonstick cooking oil. Divide the chicken wings between drawers.
4. Select zone 1 and pair it with "AIR FRY" at 200°C for 33 minutes. Select "MATCH" followed by the "START/STOP" button.
5. At the halfway point, turn the wings over, and baste them with the reserved marinade.

Cheesy Polenta Stacks

Servings: 6
Prep time: 10 minutes / Cook time: 30 minutes

Ingredients
- 350ml vegetable broth
- 150g quick-cook polenta
- 2 tsp soy butter
- Sea salt and ground black pepper, to taste
- 1 tsp cayenne pepper
- 150g cheddar cheese, sliced

Preparation Instructions
1. In a saucepan, bring the vegetable broth to a rapid boil. Immediately turn the heat to a medium-low; gradually and carefully, stir in the polenta, butter, salt, black pepper, and cayenne pepper.
2. Let it simmer, for about 5 minutes, uncovered, whisking continuously to avoid lumps. Pour your polenta into a deep baking tray and let it cool completely.
3. Then, transfer the baking tray to your fridge until well-chilled. Once the polenta is chilled, cut it into squares, using a sharp oiled knife.
4. Insert the crisper plates in both drawers and spray them with cooking oil. Arrange polenta squares on the crisper plates.
5. Select zone 1 and pair it with "AIR FRY" at 190°C for 30 minutes. Select "MATCH" to duplicate settings across both zones. Press the "START/STOP" button.
6. When zone 1 time reaches 10 minutes, turn the polenta squares over and brush them with nonstick cooking oil; reinsert the drawers to continue cooking.
7. When zone 1 time reaches 20 minutes, turn the polenta squares over and top them with cheese slices; reinsert the drawers to continue cooking.

Chapter 6: Vegan and Vegetarian Recipes

Crispy Air Fryer Tofu Nuggets

Serves: 2-4
Prep time: 30 Mins

Ingredients:
- 400 g block of extra-firm tofu
- 60 g all-purpose flour
- 1 tsp garlic powder
- 1 tsp paprika
- 1/2 tsp salt
- 1/4 tsp black pepper
- 2 eggs
- 120 g Panko breadcrumbs

Preparation Instructions:
1. Preheat the air fryer to 375°F (190°C).
2. Cut tofu into small bite-sized pieces and pat dry with paper towels.
3. Mix flour, garlic powder, paprika, salt, and pepper in a bowl.
4. In another bowl, whisk eggs together.
5. Dip each tofu piece in the flour mixture, then the egg mixture, and finally, coat in Panko breadcrumbs.
6. Place the tofu pieces in a single layer in the air fryer basket and spray lightly with cooking oil.
7. Cook for 10-12 minutes, flipping halfway through, until golden brown and crispy.
8. Serve hot with your favorite dipping sauce.

Sweet Potato Fries with Garlic Aioli

Serves: 2-4
Prep time: 19 Mins

Ingredients:
- 2 large sweet potatoes
- 2 tbsp cornstarch
- 1 tsp garlic powder
- 1 tsp smoked paprika
- 1/2 tsp salt
- 1/4 tsp black pepper
- 2 tbsp olive oil
- 120ml mayonnaise
- 1 tbsp lemon juice
- 2 cloves garlic, minced

Preparation Instructions:
1. Preheat the air fryer to 375°F (190°C).
2. Peel and cut sweet potatoes into thin fries.
3. Mix cornstarch, garlic powder, smoked paprika, salt, and black pepper in a bowl.
4. Toss sweet potato fries in olive oil, then coat in cornstarch mixture.
5. Place the fries in a single layer in the air fryer basket and spray lightly with cooking oil.
6. Cook for 10-12 minutes, shaking the basket halfway through, until crispy and tender.
7. Mix mayonnaise, lemon juice, and minced garlic in a small bowl to make garlic aioli.
8. Serve hot sweet potato fries with garlic aioli for dipping.

Spicy Buffalo Cauliflower Bites

Serves: 2-4
Prep time: 20 Mins

Ingredients:
- 1 head cauliflower, cut into bite-sized pieces
- 60 g all-purpose flour
- 1 tsp garlic powder
- 1 tsp smoked paprika
- 1/2 tsp salt
- 1/4 tsp black pepper
- 2 eggs
- 120ml buffalo sauce
- 2 tbsp butter, melted

Preparation Instructions:
1. Preheat the air fryer to 375°F (190°C).
2. Mix flour, garlic powder, smoked paprika, salt, and pepper in a bowl.
3. In another bowl, whisk eggs together.
4. Dip each cauliflower piece in the flour mixture, then the egg mixture, and place in the air fryer basket.
5. Cook for 8-10 minutes, shaking the basket halfway through, until slightly browned and tender.

6. In a small bowl, mix buffalo sauce and melted butter.
7. Remove cauliflower from the air fryer and toss in the buffalo sauce mixture until well coated.
8. Return the cauliflower to the air fryer basket and cook for 2-3 minutes until crispy.
9. Serve hot with celery sticks and blue cheese dressing.

Air Fryer Onion Rings

Serves: 4
Prep time: 17 Mins

Ingredients:
- 2 large sweet onions
- 120 g all-purpose flour
- 1 tsp garlic powder
- 1 tsp smoked paprika
- 1 tsp salt
- 1/2 tsp black pepper
- 2 eggs
- 60 g panko breadcrumbs
- Cooking spray

Preparation Instructions:
1. Preheat the air fryer to 375°F.
2. Slice the onions into thick rings and separate them.
3. Mix the flour, garlic powder, smoked paprika, salt, and black pepper in a shallow dish.
4. In another shallow dish, whisk the eggs.
5. In a third shallow dish, place the panko breadcrumbs.
6. Coat each onion ring in the flour mixture, dip it in the egg mixture, and coat it with the breadcrumbs.
7. Place the onion rings in a single layer in the air fryer basket, lightly spray them with cooking spray, and cook for 8-10 minutes.
8. Flip the onion rings and cook for another 3-5 minutes or until golden brown and crispy.
9. Repeat the process until all the onion rings are cooked.

Mediterranean Chickpea Burgers

Serves: 4
Prep time: 30 Mins

Ingredients:
- 2 cans chickpeas, drained and rinsed
- 1/2 red onion, finely chopped
- 60 g parsley, chopped

- 50 g breadcrumbs
- 1 egg
- 1 tsp cumin
- 1 tsp smoked paprika
- 1/2 tsp salt
- 1/4 tsp black pepper
- 4 burger buns
- Toppings: lettuce, tomato, hummus, cucumber, red onion, tzatziki sauce

Preparation Instructions:
1. Preheat the oven to 400°F.
2. In a large bowl, mash the chickpeas with a fork or potato masher until they are chunky.
3. Add the red onion, parsley, breadcrumbs, egg, cumin, smoked paprika, salt, and black pepper to the chickpeas and mix well.
4. Form the mixture into 4 patties.
5. Place the patties on a baking sheet lined with parchment paper and bake for 15-20 minutes or until golden brown and crispy.
6. Toast the burger buns and assemble the burgers with toppings of your choice.

Vegan Air Fryer Falafel

Serves: 4
Prep time: 25 Mins

Ingredients:
- 2 cans chickpeas, drained and rinsed
- 1/2 red onion(60 g), finely chopped
- 120 ml parsley, chopped
- 120 ml cilantro, chopped
- 30 g flour
- 1 tsp cumin
- 1 tsp coriander
- 1/2 tsp salt
- 1/4 tsp black pepper
- Cooking spray

Preparation Instructions:
1. Preheat the air fryer to 375°F.
2. In a food processor, pulse the chickpeas, red onion, parsley, cilantro, flour, cumin, coriander, salt, and black pepper until finely chopped but not pureed.
3. Form the mixture into small balls.
4. Place the balls in the air fryer basket in a single

layer and lightly spray them with cooking spray.

5. Cook for 10-12 minutes or until golden brown and crispy.

6. Repeat the process until all the falafel balls are cooked.

7. Serve with hummus, pita bread, and fresh vegetables.

Crispy Zucchini Fries

Number of Servings: 4
Prep time: 18 Mins

Ingredients:
- 2 medium zucchinis, sliced into thin sticks
- 120g of all-purpose flour90
- 2 teaspoons of paprika
- 2 teaspoons of garlic powder
- 1 teaspoon of salt
- 1 teaspoon of black pepper
- 2 eggs, lightly beaten
- 120 g Panko breadcrumbs

Preparation Instructions:
1. Preheat the air fryer to 375°F (190°C).
2. Mix the flour, paprika, garlic powder, salt, and pepper in a shallow bowl.
3. Beat the eggs in a separate shallow bowl.
4. Put the Panko breadcrumbs in a third shallow bowl.
5. Dip each zucchini stick into the flour mixture, then the egg mixture, and then coat it with Panko breadcrumbs.
6. Place the breaded zucchini sticks in the air fryer basket, ensuring they do not touch each other.
7. Lightly spray the zucchini sticks with cooking spray.
8. Cook for 8-10 minutes or until golden brown and crispy, flipping the zucchini sticks halfway through cooking.
9. Serve hot with your favorite dipping sauce.

Vegan BBQ "Pulled Pork" Jackfruit Sandwiches

Number of Servings: 4
Prep time: 45 Mins

Ingredients:
- 2 cans of young green jackfruit in water, drained

and rinsed
- 1 onion, chopped
- 2 cloves of garlic, minced
- 240 ml BBQ sauce
- 1 tablespoon of olive oil
- Salt and black pepper to taste
- 4 vegan burger buns

Preparation Instructions:
1. Heat the olive oil in a large skillet over medium-high heat.
2. Add the chopped onion and minced garlic to the skillet and sauté until soft and translucent.
3. Add the drained and rinsed jackfruit to the skillet and sauté for 5-7 minutes until it browns.
4. Add the BBQ sauce to the skillet and stir well to coat the jackfruit.
5. Reduce the heat to low and simmer for 20-30 minutes until the jackfruit is tender and the BBQ sauce has thickened.
6. Use two forks to shred the jackfruit into a "pulled pork" texture.
7. Toast the vegan burger buns and fill them with the "pulled pork" jackfruit.
8. Serve hot with your favorite vegan coleslaw or pickles.

Vegan Air Fryer Buffalo Tofu Bites

Number of Servings: 4
Prep time: 40 Mins

Ingredients:
- 1 block of extra firm tofu, drained and pressed
- 60 g all-purpose flour
- 1/2 teaspoon of garlic powder
- 1/2 teaspoon of salt
- 1/4 teaspoon of black pepper
- 120 ml plant-based milk
- 55 g of Panko breadcrumbs
- 120 g buffalo sauce

Preparation Instructions:
1. Preheat the air fryer to 375°F (190°C).
2. Cut the pressed tofu into small bite-sized pieces.
3. Mix together the flour, garlic powder, salt, and pepper in a shallow bowl.
4. Pour the plant-based milk into a separate shallow bowl.

5. Put the Panko breadcrumbs in a third shallow bowl.
6. Dip each tofu bite into the flour mixture, then the plant-based milk, and then coat it with Panko breadcrumbs.
7. Place the breaded tofu bites in the air fryer basket, ensuring they do not touch each other.
8. Lightly spray the tofu bites with cooking spray.

Air Fryer Broccoli Tots

Number of Serves: 4
Prep time: 20 Mins

Ingredients:
- 470 ml cooked broccoli florets
- 120 g panko breadcrumbs
- 60 g grated parmesan cheese
- 1/2 teaspoon garlic powder
- 1/2 teaspoon onion powder
- Salt and pepper to taste
- 2 eggs, beaten

Preparation Instructions:
1. Preheat your air fryer to 400°F (200°C).
2. Place the cooked broccoli florets in a food processor and pulse until finely chopped.
3. Combine the chopped broccoli, panko breadcrumbs, parmesan cheese, garlic powder, onion powder, salt, and pepper in a mixing bowl.
4. Add the beaten eggs and mix well.
5. Form the mixture into small tots using your hands.
6. Place the tots into the air fryer basket, ensuring they are not touching each other.
7. Air fry for 10-12 minutes, flipping them halfway through cooking until they are crispy and golden brown.
8. Serve immediately with your favorite dipping sauce.

Vegan "Fried" Pickles

Serves: 4
Prep time: 17 Mins

Ingredients:
- 240 ml dill pickle slices
- 64 g all-purpose flour
- 1/2 teaspoon garlic powder
- 1/2 teaspoon smoked paprika
- Salt and pepper to taste
- 120 ml unsweetened almond milk
- 85 g panko breadcrumbs

Preparation Instructions:
1. Preheat your air fryer to 400°F (200°C).
2. Whisk together the flour, garlic powder, smoked paprika, salt, and pepper in a shallow bowl.
3. Pour the almond milk into another shallow bowl.
4. Place the panko breadcrumbs in a third shallow bowl.
5. Dip each pickle slice in the flour mixture, the almond milk, and the panko breadcrumbs, ensuring they are coated evenly.
6. Place the coated pickles in the air fryer basket, ensuring they are not touching each other.
7. Air fry for 8-10 minutes, flipping them halfway through cooking until they are crispy and golden brown.
8. Serve immediately with your favorite dipping sauce.

Air Fryer Veggie "Fried" Rice

Number of Serves: 4
Prep time: 20 Mins

Ingredients:
- 480 ml cooked brown rice
- 1 tablespoon vegetable oil
- 1 onion, diced
- 2 garlic cloves, minced
- 1 tablespoon grated ginger
- 1 red bell pepper, diced
- 160 g frozen peas and carrots
- 2 tablespoons soy sauce
- 1 teaspoon sesame oil
- Salt and pepper to taste
- 2 eggs, beaten (optional)

Preparation Instructions:
1. Preheat your air fryer to 400°F (200°C).
2. In a large skillet, heat the vegetable oil over medium-high heat.
3. Add the onion, garlic, and ginger and sauté until fragrant, about 2 minutes.
4. Add the red bell pepper and frozen peas and carrots and cook for another 5 minutes, until the vegetables are tender.
5. Add the cooked brown rice, soy sauce, sesame

oil, salt, and pepper and stir until well combined.

6. Optional: Push the veggie rice mixture to one side of the skillet and add the beaten eggs to the other side. Scramble the eggs until cooked, then mix them into the veggie rice.

7. Transfer the veggie rice mixture to the air fryer basket, spreading it in an even layer.

8. Air fry for 5-8 minutes, until the rice is crispy and heated

Vegan Air Fryer Taquitos

Number of Serves: 4
Prep time: 25 Mins

Ingredients:
- 1 can of black beans, drained and rinsed (about 400 g)
- 70 g of frozen corn
- 30 g of diced red onion
- 15 g of chopped fresh cilantro
- 2 tablespoons of fresh lime juice
- 1 teaspoon of cumin
- 1/2 teaspoon of chili powder
- 1/2 teaspoon of garlic powder
- 1/4 teaspoon of salt
- 12 small corn tortillas
- 25 g of vegan cheese, shredded
- Cooking spray

Preparation Instructions:
1. Preheat the air fryer to 400°F.
2. Combine the black beans, frozen corn, red onion, cilantro, lime juice, cumin, chili powder, garlic powder, and salt in a medium bowl.
3. Wrap the corn tortillas in a damp paper towel and microwave for 20 seconds to soften.
4. Place 2 tablespoons of the bean mixture and 1 teaspoon of vegan cheese in the center of each tortilla.
5. Roll the tortilla tightly and place it seam-side down in the air fryer basket.
6. Repeat with the remaining tortillas and bean mixture.
7. Spray the taquitos with cooking spray.
8. Cook in the air fryer for 10-12 minutes, flipping halfway through, until golden brown and crispy.
9. Serve with your favorite toppings, such as avocado, salsa, or vegan sour cream.

Air Fryer Eggplant Parmesan

Serves: 4
Prep time: 25 Mins

Ingredients:
- 1 large eggplant, sliced into 1/2-inch rounds
- 120 g of all-purpose flour
- 240 g of panko breadcrumbs
- 50 g of vegan Parmesan cheese, grated
- 1 teaspoon of dried basil
- 1 teaspoon of dried oregano
- 1/2 teaspoon of garlic powder
- 1/4 teaspoon of salt
- 2 tablespoons of olive oil
- 240 ml of marinara sauce
- 70 g of vegan mozzarella cheese, shredded

Preparation Instructions:
1. Preheat the air fryer to 400°F.
2. Place the flour in a shallow dish.
3. Combine the panko breadcrumbs, vegan Parmesan cheese, basil, oregano, garlic powder, and salt in a separate shallow dish.
4. Dip each eggplant slice in the flour, then press the breadcrumbs onto the eggplant to coat in the breadcrumb mixture.
5. Place the coated eggplant slices in a single layer in the air fryer basket.
6. Drizzle the olive oil over the eggplant slices.
7. Cook in the air fryer for 8-10 minutes, flipping halfway through, until the eggplant is tender and the breadcrumbs are golden brown and crispy.
8. Spoon the marinara sauce over the eggplant slices and sprinkle with vegan mozzarella cheese.
9. Cook for 2-3 minutes until the cheese is melted and bubbly.
10. Serve hot with your favorite side dish.

Crispy Air Fryer Brussels Sprouts

Serves: 2
Prep time: 22 Mins

Ingredients:
- 450 g fresh Brussels sprouts
- 1 tbsp olive oil
- 1 tsp garlic powder

- 1/2 tsp salt
- 1/4 tsp black pepper

Preparation Instructions:
1. Preheat the air fryer to 375°F.
2. Wash and dry the Brussels sprouts.
3. Cut off the stems and slice them in half.
4. In a large bowl, toss the Brussels sprouts with olive oil, garlic powder, salt, and black pepper.
5. Place the Brussels sprouts in the air fryer basket in a single layer.
6. Cook for 12-15 minutes or until crispy and golden brown.
7. Shake the basket every 5 minutes to ensure even cooking.
8. Try to serve immediately.

Vegan Air Fryer Potato Skins

Serves: 4
Prep time: 1Hr 10 Mins

Ingredients:
- 4 medium-sized russet potatoes
- 1 tbsp olive oil
- 1/2 tsp garlic powder
- 1/2 tsp salt
- 1/4 tsp black pepper
- 60 g vegan cheese shreds
- 2 tbsp vegan bacon bits
- 2 green onions, chopped

Preparation Instructions:
1. Preheat the air fryer to 375°F.
2. Wash and dry the potatoes.
3. Pierce each potato several times with a fork and place them in the air fryer basket.
4. Cook for 30-35 minutes or until they are tender.
5. Let the potatoes cool for 10-15 minutes.
6. Cut each potato in half lengthwise and scoop out the flesh, leaving about 1/4 inch of flesh in each half.
7. Brush the potato skins with olive oil and sprinkle with garlic powder, salt, and black pepper.
8. Place the potato skins in the air fryer basket and cook for 5-7 minutes or until they are crispy and golden brown.
9. Remove the potato skins from the air fryer and sprinkle with vegan cheese shreds and bacon bits.

10. Place the potato skins back in the air fryer and cook for 2-3 minutes or until the cheese is melted.
11. Top with chopped green onions and serve immediately.

Air Fryer Falafel Burgers

Serves: 4
Prep time: 23 Mins

Ingredients:
- 1 can (425 ml) chickpeas, drained and rinsed
- 8g fresh parsley leaves
- 4g fresh cilantro leaves
- 40g chopped onion
- 2 garlic cloves, minced
- 1 tsp ground cumin
- 1 tsp ground coriander
- 1/2 tsp salt
- 1/4 tsp black pepper
- 30g all-purpose flour
- 1 tbsp olive oil
- 4 whole wheat burger buns
- 4 lettuce leaves
- 4 tomato slices
- 4 tbsp hummus

Preparation Instructions:
1. Preheat the air fryer to 375°F.
2. In a food processor, pulse the chickpeas, parsley, cilantro, onion, garlic, cumin, coriander, salt, and black pepper until the mixture is finely chopped but not pureed.
3. Add the flour and pulse until combined.
4. Divide the mixture into 4 equal portions and shape them into burgers.
5. Brush each burger with olive oil.
6. Place the burgers in the air fryer basket and cook for 12-15 minutes or until they are crispy and golden brown.
7. Toast the burger buns.
8. Assemble the burgers by placing a

Vegan Air Fryer Tater Tots

Servings: 4-6
Prep time: 25 Mins

Ingredients:
- 900g russet potatoes, peeled and grated

- 1/2 teaspoon garlic powder
- 1/2 teaspoon onion powder
- 1/2 teaspoon paprika
- 1/2 teaspoon salt
- 1/4 teaspoon black pepper
- 2 tablespoons all-purpose flour
- 2 tablespoons cornstarch
- Cooking spray

Preparation Instructions:
1. Preheat the air fryer to 400°F.
2. Place the grated potatoes in a clean kitchen towel and squeeze the excess liquid.
3. In a large mixing bowl, combine the grated potatoes with garlic powder, onion powder, paprika, salt, black pepper, all-purpose flour, and cornstarch. Mix well until all Ingredients are evenly distributed.
4. Spray the air fryer basket with cooking spray.
5. Using a cookie scoop or tablespoon, form small tater tots and place them in the air fryer basket.
6. Spray the tater tots with cooking spray.
7. Air fry the tater tots for 12-15 minutes, flipping halfway through cooking until golden brown and crispy.
8. Serve hot and enjoy!

Air Fryer Stuffed Mushrooms

Servings: 4-6
Prep time: 20 Mins

Ingredients:
- 20 medium-sized mushrooms, cleaned and stemmed
- 30g breadcrumbs
- 30ml grated Parmesan cheese
- 4g chopped fresh parsley
- 20g chopped onion
- 2 cloves garlic, minced
- 3 tablespoons olive oil
- Salt and pepper to taste

Preparation Instructions:
1. Preheat the air fryer to 375°F.
2. In a medium mixing bowl, combine breadcrumbs, Parmesan cheese, parsley, onion, garlic, and olive oil. Mix well until all Ingredients are evenly distributed.

3. Stuff each mushroom cap with the breadcrumb mixture, pressing down gently to ensure it sticks.
4. Place the stuffed mushrooms in the air fryer basket.
5. Air fry the mushrooms for 10-12 minutes until the tops are golden brown and crispy.
6. Serve hot and enjoy!

Vegetarian Burgers

Serves 4
Prep time: 10 minutes / Cook time: 18 minutes

Ingredients:
- 300g millet, soaked overnight and rinsed
- 300g canned red kidney beans, drained and rinsed
- 1 small carrot, trimmed and grated
- 1 medium onion, finely chopped
- 2 garlic cloves, pressed
- 2 tbsp BBQ sauce
- Sea salt and ground black pepper, to taste
- 100g tortilla chips, crushed

Preparation Instructions:
1. Insert the crisper plates in both drawers and spray them with cooking oil.
2. In a mixing bowl, thoroughly combine all the Ingredients. Shape the mixture into 6 patties and arrange them in the drawers.
3. Select zone 1 and pair it with "AIR FRY" at 180°C for 18 minutes. Select "MATCH" to duplicate settings across both zones. Press the "START/STOP" button.
4. When zone 1 time reaches 10 minutes, turn the burgers over and reinsert the drawers to continue cooking.
5. Serve warm burgers in buns with the topping of choice.

Vegan Bean Burgers

Serves 4
Prep time: 10 minutes / Cook time: 20 minutes

Ingredients:
- 1 (400g) can red kidney beans, rinsed and drained
- 300g buckwheat, soaked overnight and rinsed
- 1 small bunch of coriander
- 1 medium onion, chopped
- 100g breadcrumbs
- Sea salt and ground black pepper, to taste

- 1 tsp cumin seeds
- 150g tub salsa

Preparation Instructions:

1. Insert the crisper plates in both drawers and spray them with cooking oil.
2. In your blender or a food processor, thoroughly combine all the Ingredients. Shape the mixture into 6 patties and spray them with nonstick cooking oil. Now, arrange them in the lightly-greased drawers.
3. Select zone 1 and pair it with "AIR FRY" at 190°C for 20 minutes. Select "MATCH" to duplicate settings across both zones. Press the "START/STOP" button.
4. When zone 1 time reaches 10 minutes, turn the burgers over, spray them with cooking oil on the other side, and reinsert the drawers to continue cooking.
5. Serve warm patties in hamburger buns with toppings of choice.

Vegan Shish Kebab with Broccoli

Serves 4

Prep time: 50 minutes / Cook time: 10 minutes

Ingredients

- 200g brown rice, soaked overnight and rinsed
- 1 tsp olive oil
- 200 g canned or cooked kidney beans, rinsed and drained
- 1 garlic clove
- 2 spring onions
- 30g BBQ sauce
- Sea salt and ground black pepper, to taste
- 1/2 tsp ground coriander
- 50g breadcrumbs
- 1 (400g) head broccoli, cut into 2.5cm florets
- 1 tbsp olive oil

Preparation Instructions

1. Insert a crisper plate into zone 1. Spray the crisper plate with nonstick cooking oil.
2. In a medium saucepan, cook brown rice with 400ml of water (or vegetable broth) and olive oil for about 45 minutes, until it has absorbed the water.
3. Add the rice, along with the beans, garlic, onions, BBQ sauce, and spices to a bowl of your food processor. Process the Ingredients for about 30 seconds. Shape the mixture into 4 kebabs.
4. Add the breadcrumbs to a shallow dish and then, roll the kebabs over the breadcrumbs, pressing to adhere.
5. Now, spray the kebabs with nonstick cooking oil and then, place them in the lightly-greased zone 1 drawer. Toss broccoli florets with 1 tablespoon of olive oil, salt, and pepper to taste; place them in the zone 2 drawer.
6. Select zone 1 and pair it with "AIR FRY" at 180°C for 15 minutes. Select zone 2 and pair it with "ROAST" at 190°C for 9 minutes. Select "SYNC" followed by the "START/STOP" button.
7. When zone 1 time reaches 8 minutes, turn the kebabs over using silicone-tipped tongs. Reinsert the drawer to continue cooking. Serve warm kebabs with roasted broccoli florets and enjoy!

Chapter 7: Family favourites

Festive Yorkshire Puddings

Serves 6 (recipe scalable)
Prep time: 10 minutes / Cook time: 17 minutes

Ingredients

- 1 Large Egg
- 180g of all-purpose flour
- 180ml milk
- 180ml water
- ¾ tsp table salt
- 1 cal olive fry spray

Preparation Instructions

1. You will need to prepare the Yorkshire Pudding by mixing the Ingredients, and placing them into the refrigerator for 1 hour
2. Pour 1 tbsp olive oil into empty ramekins, then place them in the ninja foodi zones
3. Preheat air fryer to 200°C for 6 minutes
4. Pour the Pudding mixture into the ramekins
5. Select the zone settings and pair it to 'BAKE' at 200°C for 18 minutes
6. Retrieve the Yorkshire puddings and serve them as part of your Sunday or Christmas Dinner

Christmas Bomb Cake Duo

Serves 4
Prep time: 5 minutes / Cook time: 15 minutes

Ingredients

- 1 x 227g Belgium chocolate bomb cake
- 1 x 227g chocolate orange bomb cake
- 1cal olive fry spray

Preparation Instructions

1. Preheat the ninja foodi to 180°C for 5 minutes
2. Place 1 bomb cake in each zone draw of the ninja foodi
3. Select the zone setting and pair it with 'BAKE' at 180°C for 6 minutes
4. Press 'MATCH' followed by 'STOP/START' to cook the cake and milk the fillings
5. Retrieve the cakes, cut in half to see the filings ooze out, then serve (1 cake served 2)

Mini Victoria Sponge Cake

Serves 7-8
Prep time: 30 minutes / Cook time: 30 minutes

Ingredients

- 4 large eggs
- 150g of brown sugar
- ¼ tsp Vanilla Extract
- 130g cake flour

For filling/To serve

- 100g butter, softened
- 140g icing sugar, sifted
- 400g strawberry Jam (real berries)
- 8 strawberries, halved

Preparation Instructions

1. Using a stand mixer, whisk the eggs, brown sugar and vanilla extract for 20 minutes, in order to create a 'spongy' texture
2. Sift the cake flour into this newly formed mixture and fold it continuously until the lumps have been removed
3. Saturate 7-8 bake pots with 1 cal olive fry spray, then fill them with the cake mixture
4. Cover the bake pots with tin foil and put a 1 cm incision in the centre to act as a vent whilst baking
5. Divide the cake pots amongst both draws amongst the dual zone, then pair them to 'BAKE' at 150°C for 30 minutes
6. Press 'MATCH' and 'START/STOP' to bake the sponge base
7. Once complete, set to cool for 10 minutes, then horizontally in the centre of the sponge cake to create two layers (lower and upper)
8. Beat the butter on top of the lower layer (cake centre)
9. Sift half of the icing sugar and spread it on top if the butter
10. Dollop and spread the strawberry jam on top of the icing
11. Sift the other half of the icing sugar at the bottom of the upper cake layer
12. Place the upper layer of the sponge cake on top of the lower layer, then top each mini sponge cake with 2 strawberry halves
13. Set the mini victoria sponge cakes on the dinner

table as a dessert for the family to enjoy

Jam Roly Poly Pudding Topped With Custard

Serves 8
Prep time: 3 minutes / Cook time: 8 minutes

Ingredients
- 2 ready roly poly puddings
- 250ml ready custard

Preparation Instructions
1. Remove the roly poly puddings from the packet and place 1 in each zone of the dual zone
2. Pair the zones with 'BAKE' at 190°C for 7 minutes
3. Press 'MATCH' then 'START/STOP' to begin cooking the roly polys
4. Once cooked, take the roly poly puddings out of the dual zone then cut each one into 4 quarters
5. Place each quarter in a small bowl and top with some custard to serve

Camembert Wreath

Serves 4
Prep time: 3 minutes / Cook time: 15 minutes

Ingredients
- 600g wreath bread
- 300g Camembert cheese (for dipping)

Preparation Instructions
1. Preheat the duel zone to 180°C for 5 minutes
2. Slice the wreath into 4 quarters and place them in the zone 1 draw of the duel zone
3. Place the camembert cheese in an oven proof bowl, then slot it into the zone 2 draw
4. Select zone 1 and pair it to 'BAKE' for 10 minutes, then select zone 2 and pair it to 'ROAST' for 15 minutes
5. Press 'SYNC' followed by 'START/STOP' to start cooking the food contents
6. Flip the bread and stir the camembert half way through the cooking duration
7. Once complete Retrieve the food content and plate them up to serve

Mini Oreo Cheesecakes

Serves: 10 mini cheesecakes
Prep time: 45 minutes / Cook time: 30 minutes

Ingredients
- 10 Oreos
- 250 g cream cheese
- 1 beaten egg
- 64 g chopped Mars bars
- Whipped cream (to serve)

Preparation Instructions
1. Line the air fryer tray with muffin cases.
2. Split the Oreo cookies and place one half cream side up in each muffin case.
3. Beat the cream cheese and add the egg.
4. Melt all the Mars bars and add to the cream cheese.
5. Spoon 2 tablespoons of the mixture onto each Oreo cookie in the muffin cases.
6. Top with the other half of the Oreo cookies.
7. Air fry in batches for 8-10 minutes at 160 degrees Celsius.
8. Serve topped with a little whipped cream.

Dehydrated Fruit

Serves: 20+
Prep time: 5 minutes / Cook time: 6 minutes

Ingredients
- 2 apples, thinly sliced
- 2 oranges, thinly sliced
- 2 lemons, thinly sliced
- 2 pears, thinly sliced
- 2 passion fruits, thinly sliced
- 2 apricots, thinly sliced
- 2 peaches, thinly slices

Preparation Instructions
1. Load up nothing zone draws with sliced fruit
2. Select the ninja zones and pair them with 'DEHYDRATE' at 50°C for 6 hrs.
3. Press 'MATCH' followed by 'START/STOP' to dehydration process
4. Retrieve the dehydrated fruits and place them on a fruit dish to serve

Caramelised Figs

Serves:4
Prep time: 5 minutes / Cook time: 11 minutes

Ingredients
- 600g figs

- 35g brown sugar
- 1 tsp ground cinnamon

Preparation Instructions

1. Preheat the air fryer at 180°C for 3 minutes
2. Using a sharp knife, remove the stalks of the figs and place them in a mixing bowl
3. In another small bowl, combine brown sugar and cinnamon using a fork.
4. Drizzle and massage this powder based mixture on the figs
5. Using some kitchen tongs, place the figs in both zone draws of for dual zone
6. Select the 'BAKE' function and increase the temperature to 200°C for 11 minutes
7. Press 'MATCH' followed by 'STOP/START' to caramelise the figs
8. At the 5 minute mark, give the figs a shake
9. Retrieve the caramelised figs using kitchen tongs, then serve

Grilled Peaches

Serves: 4

Prep time: 5 minutes / Cook time: 10 minutes

Ingredients

- 2 peaches
- 35 g crushed digestive biscuits
- 30 g brown sugar
- 60 g butter

Preparation Instructions

1. Remove pits from the peaches and cut into wedges.
2. Cut butter into small cubes.
3. Mix the crumbs, sugar and butter together.
4. Put the peach wedges in the airfryer.
5. Sprinkle the peaches with the crumb mixture.
6. Cook for 10 minutes at 190°C.

Cornbread Muffins

Serves: 6

Prep time: 10 minutes / Cook time: 25 minutes

Ingredients

- 50g butter, melted
- 2 scallion stalks, chopped
- 100g sweetcorn kernels
- 2 small eggs
- 50ml milk

- 140ml pot buttermilk
- 80g plain flour
- 80g polenta or cornmeal
- 1 tsp baking powder
- 30g Swiss cheese, grated

Preparation Instructions:

1. Remove a crisper plate from your Ninja Foodi. Lightly spray muffin cases with cooking oil.
2. Melt the butter in a frying pan over medium-low heat; cook scallion and corn kernels for approximately 5 minutes, until soft.
3. Add the other Ingredients and gently stir to combine. Spoon the mixture into the prepared muffin cases.
4. Add muffin cases to both drawers.
5. Select zone 1 and pair it with "BAKE" at 180°C for 25 minutes, until golden brown. Select "MATCH" to duplicate settings across both zones. Press the "START/STOP" button.

Millet Banana Porridge

Serves: 5

Prep time: 10 minutes / Cook time: 12 minutes

Ingredients

- 2 tsp coconut oil, melted
- 350g millet grains, rinsed
- 1 litre milk
- 100g dates, pitted and chopped
- 2 large bananas, peeled and mashed
- 1 tsp vanilla bean paste
- 1 cinnamon stick

Preparation Instructions:

1. Brush the inside of two oven-safe baking tins with coconut oil.
2. Tip the millet into a deep saucepan and pour in the milk; add 350ml of water and bring it to a boil. Reduce the heat to medium-low and leave to simmer for approximately 11 minutes, stirring continuously, until the millet is tender.
3. Mix the millet with the other Ingredients and spoon the mixture into the baking tins. Add the baking tins to the drawers.
4. Select zone 1 and pair it with "BAKE" at 180°C for 12 minutes. Select "MATCH" to duplicate settings across both zones. Press the "START/STOP" button.
5. When zone 1 time reaches 6 minutes, turn the baking

tin and reinsert the drawers to continue cooking.

Classic Home Made 'Fish Shop' Dinner

Serves: 4
Prep time: 15 minutes / Cook time:30 minutes

Ingredients
For Fish
- 4 Haddock fillets (250g each)
- 1 Large egg
- 80g dried breadcrumbs
- 20g grated parmesan cheese
- ¼ tsp ground pepper
- ¼ tsp sea salt
- 45g all purpose flour
- 30ml water

For Chips
- 2 Large potatoes
- 2 tbsp peanut oil
- ¼ tbsp sea salt
- ¼ tbsp ground pepper
- Vinegar

To serve/sides
- 70g curry sauce, premade
- 4 pickled eggs, premade
- 4 pickled gherkins, premade
- 4 picked onions, premade

Preparation Instructions
1. Preheat the air fryer at 200°C for 10 minutes
2. Meanwhile, peel and cut the potatoes into thick chips
3. Using a large bowl combine all of the 'For Chips' Ingredients
4. Hand toss and fold the chips, ensuring that the potato is covered in the spices, then set them aside
5. Add flour, egg and Breadcrumbs & Parmesan in 3 separate bowls
6. Treacle the fish with salt and then submerge them into flour, egg, then the breadcrumbs mix
7. Place the coated coat in zone 1 and chips in zone 2 of the duel zone air fryer
8. Select zone 1 and pair it with 'AIR FRY' at 200°C for 20 minutes
9. Select zone 2 and also pair with 'AIR FRY' at 200°C, but with a 15 minutes cooking time
10. Press 'SYNC' followed by 'STOP/START' to

air fry the fish and chips
11. Flip the fish at the 10-minute mark and shake the chips at the 7-minute mark
12. Retrieve the fish and chips, divide them amongst 4 plates
13. To accompany the fish and chips, dollop 1 tbsp of curry sauce, 1 picked egg, 1 pickled onion, and 1 pickled gherkin

Spaghetti and Meatballs

Serves: 4
Prep time: 15 minutes / Cook time: 15 minutes

Ingredients
- 2 Large eggs
- 2 Teaspoons of Balsamic Vinegar
- 1/4 Teaspoon of salt
- 1/4 Teaspoon of black pepper
- 115 g of breadcrumbs
- 4 cloves of garlic (two chopped and two grated)
- 90 g Parmesan cheese
- 170 g chopped flat-leaf Parsley
- 230 g of minced beef
- 340g spaghetti
- 450g cherry tomatoes
- 1 Tablespoon of olive oil
- 190g Marinara sauce

Preparation Instructions
1. Whisk eggs, vinegar, and 1/4 teaspoon of each salt and pepper in a big basin. Add the breadcrumbs, then stir and wait one minute. Garlic, Parmesan, and parsley are all stirred in after that. Add the beef, then blend gently.
2. 20 balls of the beef mixture, each measuring about 1 1/2 inches in diameter, should be formed (balls can touch, but should not be stacked; cook in batches if necessary). Meatballs should be air-fried for 5 minutes at 200 degrees Celsius.
3. Meanwhile, cook spaghetti per package directions.
4. Combine oil, 1/4 teaspoon of salt, and 1/4 teaspoon of pepper in a bowl with the tomatoes and chopped garlic. When the meatballs are thoroughly cooked, scatter them over and continue air-frying for an additional 5 to 6 minutes.
5. Toss spaghetti gently with the meatballs, tomatoes, and marinara. If preferred, garnish with Parmesan and basil before serving.

Printed in Great Britain
by Amazon